DEVOTIONAL
EDITION

Heaven

YOUR REAL HOME

JONI EARECKSON TADA

ZONDERVAN™

GRAND RAPIDS, MICHIGAN 49530

ZONDERVAN™

Heaven
Copyright © 1996 by Zondervan

ISBN 0-310-24165-0

Excerpts taken from: *Heaven* Copyright © 1995 by Joni Eareckson Tada. Published by Zondervan, a division of HarperCollins Publishers.

This book is printed on acid-free paper.

Project Editor: Sarah Hupp
Interior Design: Melissa Elenbaas

Printed in the United States of America

01 02 03 04 05 /❖ DC/ 8 7 6 5 4 3 2 1

CONTENTS

PART 1

WHAT'S SO GREAT ABOUT HEAVEN?

If God hath made this world so fair
Where sin and death abound,
How beautiful beyond compare
Will paradise be found.

—JAMES MONTGOMERY

I love thinking and reading about heaven. I have to confess, though, I've never succeeded in painting a picture of heaven. People have asked me why, and I haven't come up with a good answer, except to say that heaven defies the blank canvas of the artist. The best I can offer are scenes of breathtaking mountains or clouds that halfway reflect something of heaven's majesty. I'm never quite able to achieve the effect.

And neither is earth. Actual mountains and clouds are exalting, but even the most beautiful displays of earth's glory—towering thunderheads above a wheat field or the view of the Grand Canyon from the south rim—are only rough sketches of heaven. Earth's best is only a dim reflection, a preliminary rendering of the glory that will one day be revealed.

Yet I've noticed as I've flipped through the pages of Scripture—our best resource about heaven—that its language is cryptic. You almost have to crack heaven's hieroglyphics before any of it makes sense. How can we pursue heaven through so much confusion or consider our future "marvelous" if we keep stumbling over word pictures of crowns and thrones?

These things only seem to be deterrents. They are actually incentives. The symbols Scripture uses of palms, crowns, streets of gold, and seas of glass are just that—symbols. They never quite satisfy our curiosity about heaven, and they're not meant to. They are only shadowy images of the real thing, as well as guides and signposts that point us in the right direction to show us the way home.

That's what the following pages are. Guides and signposts to point you to heaven, the real home of our heart and spirit. Like stealing a tiny sip of stew before dinner, it's meant to be a foretaste of what to expect when you get to the banquet table. Tune into heaven's melody. The real song is about to break into a heavenly symphony, and its prelude is only a few moments away.

A HEAVENLY CHORD

On what were [earth's] footings set, or who laid its cornerstone—while the morning stars sang together and all the angels shouted for joy?

—Job 38:6-7

I huddled against the cold air to listen to my neighbor's whistling pine trees and gaze at the thin slice of moon smiling on the horizon. My eyes scanned the canopy of stars above to locate the constellation Ursa Major. —I knew the Big Dipper was part of it, but having only recently memorized it from a book, I had never seen the whole thing.

I searched and searched, and suddenly, there it was, the familiar arrangement of stars spread out grand and glorious across one-fourth of the sky. I had no idea it was so *big*. Nor had I realized how beautiful.

I shivered, feeling small and swallowed up underneath the starry dome that seemed to reverberate with a song. Yes, I could have sworn I heard a song. Was it the faint tune of a hymn in my heart? Was it the morning stars singing together? I don't know, but the song struck a chord in me, like a tuning fork resonating in my soul. The stars and music took my breath away, and before the cold drove me indoors, my heart broke with joy, and I whispered toward the sky, "Jesus, I'm coming home; I belong up there."

I wheeled out of that moment, through the garage door, and into the kitchen. The fluorescent light made me squint as I nudged the door shut. I breathed in the aroma of dinner cooking. The house was warm and softly lit, the television was droning in the living room, and my husband, Ken, was in the hallway talking to a friend on the phone.

Outside I had touched a moment of great happiness and wisdom, but I knew I was incapable of holding onto that heavenly moment. Few are skilled at holding themselves in a state of listening to heaven's music.

Ordinary things—like kitchen pots clattering, telephones ringing, and TV commercials about frozen food and dishwashing detergent—drown out the song. It is too delicate to compete against mundane things. The music and the moment fades, and we become our ordinary selves, leaving the child outside, and shelving our fascination with the moon, the stars, and the night wind. We consign heavenly thoughts to some other time. Yet we live in the powerful memory of those moments.

Rather than let that song retire in the presence of mundane things like scratchy AM radios and grinding dishwashers, I hope the following pages will help you see something far, far beyond the constellation of Ursa Major.

LORD, I THANK YOU for the promise of heaven and the unexpected moments when you touch my heartstrings with that longing for my eternal home. Cause me to look beyond my everyday experiences to focus on a glimpse of heaven. Help me to capture those moments with delight. Keep my ears of faith tuned to the heavenly song as you guide me each day. ✐

A HEAVENLY ECHO

*Why, you do not even know what will hap-
pen tomorrow. What is your life? You are a
mist that appears for a little while and then
vanishes.*

—James 4:14

Whether we are adults or children, our best memories are usu-
ally the sort which, like a tuning fork, strike that resonant chord
in our souls. It's a song we never quite forget and recognize
immediately whenever we catch its echo. We recognize it because
it is so full of heartbreaking beauty. Like deep calling to deep, it
is stamped with His imprint; and since we bear His image, the
memory is sealed in that deepest, most profound part of us. Such
moments cast soundings and plumb the real depths of who we
are. We live in the powerful memory of those moments. And
what we hear is a heavenly echo.

We may hear the haunting echo under a night sky or even in
a symphony, a poem, or catch it in a painting. In fact, it is
singers, writers, and painters who most often try to capture the
echo, this heavenly music that compels us to sing, write, or paint
something truly beautiful.

Words and even paintings, like the one I did to go at the front of this book, can sometimes strike a resonant chord, helping us hear that ancient and heavenly song which the morning stars sang together.

Trouble is, we rarely let that fact sink in. We consign heavenly thoughts to some other time. That is, until we are stopped short by one of those brilliant nights when the air is clear like crystal and the black sky studded with a million stars. It takes such a moment to make us pause, watch our breath make little clouds in the night air.

Then we rush indoors to catch the six o'clock news or referee an argument between our kids. The heavenly moment is lost and we think, *Life doesn't seem like a mist that quickly vanishes.*

We really don't believe it's all going to end, do we? If God hadn't told us differently, we'd all think this parade of life would go on forever.

But it will end. This life is not forever, nor is it the best life that will ever be. The fact is that believers *are* headed for heaven. It is reality. And what we do here on earth has a direct bearing on how we will live there. Heaven may be as near as next year, or next week; so it makes good sense to spend some time here on earth thinking candid thoughts about that marvelous future reserved for us.

LORD, I HEAR AN ECHO, a heavenly echo. At times it is so faint that I'm not even sure that I've heard it. But you have told me that this life will be over one day and that haunting echo will become a reality. Make these heavenly moments become more real in my heart and life as I learn more about you. Let me recognize that heavenly echo for what it is—my call to come home with you. ✒

A HINT OF HEAVEN

*But our citizenship is in heaven. And we
eagerly await a Savior from there, the
Lord Jesus Christ.*

—*Philippians 3:20*

The first time I heard that haunting heavenly song, so ancient and so new, was in the summer of 1957. My family and I had packed up, piled into our old Buick, and were heading west through the country roads of Kansas. Daddy pulled the car over onto the gravel shoulder to stop by a roadside ditch so my sister could go to the bathroom. I jumped out of the sweltering backseat and wandered beside a barbed wire fence along the road. It was a chance to dry the sweat off my back, as well as to explore.

I stopped and picked up a piece of gravel, examined it, and then heaved the stone beyond the fence far out into the biggest, widest, longest field I had ever seen. It was an ocean of wheat, waves of golden grain rippling in the wind, all broad and beautiful against a brilliant blue sky. I stood and stared. A warm breeze tossed my hair. A butterfly flittered. Except for the hissing sound of summertime bugs, all was quiet, incredibly quiet.

Or was it?

I can't remember if the song came from the sky or the field, or if it was just the sound of crickets. I tried hard to listen, but instead of actually hearing notes, I felt . . . space. A wide-opened space filling my heart, as if the entire wheat field could fit into my seven-year-old soul. I rolled my head back to look up at a hawk circling overhead. The bird, sky, sun, and field were lifting me in some heavenly orchestration, lightening my heart with honesty and clarity like an American folk hymn in a major key, pure, upright, and vertical. I had never felt—or was it, heard?— such a thing. Yet as soon as I tried to grasp the haunting echo, it vanished.

I was only seven, but standing there by the barbed wire fence of a Kansas wheat field, I knew my heart had been broken by God. No, I didn't actually know Him at the time, but I wasn't so young that I couldn't sense the occasional stirrings of His Spirit. I kept staring while humming an old Sunday school favorite: "This world is not my home, I'm just a-passin' through." For me, the moment was heavenly.

Daddy honked the horn and I ran back. Our family drove away with a slightly changed little girl in the backseat. I was only a little girl, but heaven seemed so close to me then.

This world is not my home, I'm just a passing thru,
My treasures are laid up somewhere beyond the blue;
The angels beckon me from Heaven's open door,
And I can't feel at home in this world anymore.
O Lord, you know I have no friend like you.
If Heaven's not my home, then Lord what will I do?
The angels beckon me from Heaven's open door,
And I can't feel at home in this world anymore.

—Albert E. Brumley

THINK ON THESE THINGS

*Set your minds on things above,
not on earthly things.*

—*Colossians 3:2*

Everybody wants to go to heaven. We are all curious to know where it is, how it looks, who's there, and what they wear and do. I'm no exception. A few years after the 1967 diving accident in which I became paralyzed, I was fascinated to discover that one day I would no longer be paralyzed but have a new glorified body. Immediately I began imagining all the wonderful things I would do with resurrected hands and legs. Swim a couple of laps. Peel a few oranges. Sprint across fields and splash into waves, scale a few rocks and skip through meadows. Such thoughts enraptured me.

But be honest. Be like any red-blooded, right-thinking Christian with both feet planted firmly on earth. I've gotten lost in the chronological chaos, wondering how Jesus' return to earth connects with the millennium, the rapture, the judgment, and the bowls, scrolls, and trumpets in the book of Revelation. And haven't there been times when word pictures of heaven from the Bible fall flat and boring next to the breathtaking sight and thunderous roar of Niagara Falls? Or scanning the serene Colorado plains from the pinnacle of Pikes Peak? Do you sense that sometimes the musical notes of God's creation almost eclipse Ezekiel's footnotes describing things in heaven as wheels that intersect other wheels as well as move in four directions? "Their rims were high and awesome, and all four rims were full of eyes all around" (Ezekiel 1:18). *Whhaat?*

Reading about heaven in Scripture can almost sound like bad copy in a Triple A tour book:

> *A large set of pearl-studded gates will welcome you to heaven, but be careful of slippery roads that are paved with gold. Topping the list of scenic points is a sea of glass. However, local conditions preclude sunsets, sunrises, or full moons. Do not miss the spectacular New Jerusalem, a striking city of the future, employing award-winning architectural design. Marvel at its twelve foundations. Stand amazed before its twelve gates, each made of a gigantic, single pearl. For sheer spectacle, the New Jerusalem eclipses even the Emerald City of Oz.*

You can't ignore streets of gold and rainbow thrones just because they don't thrill you at first glance. They're the images God gave us—the symbols Scripture invites us to ponder. They're not deterrents to your faith, they're incentives. The Bible provides the symbols. But it is faith that makes the hieroglyphics of heaven come alive.

LORD, I ADMIT THAT my view of heaven has been a little warped by my own needs or desires. At times roaring waterfalls and breathtaking scenery thrill me more than the thoughts of heaven. Help me see heaven's symbols as clues to an amazing mystery that will ignite my heart. Help me set my mind on things above. Turn my thoughts toward heaven and you. ✒

Negative Symbols

*Then I saw a new heaven and a new earth,
for the first heaven and the first earth had
passed away, and there was no longer any sea.*

—Revelation 21:1

I'm struck that heaven is often described in terms of "no this" and "no that." No more sea. No more night. No more time. No more moon or sun. It was lost on me how so much of heaven's happiness could be described in negative terms. Why did God seem to talk about heaven in terms of what it will *not* be, rather than what it will be?

That's not all. I was also struck that the positive descriptions about what heaven is seem clumsy and ungraceful. Rainbow thrones? Streets of gold? Pearly gates? A glittering city 1,400 miles in length and as wide and high as it is long with walls 200 feet thick and made of jasper? It more closely resembled Minnesota's monolithic Mall of America. I was embarrassed to admit it, but even the descriptions about everlasting peace and eternal felicity seemed boring.

I wanted those streets of gold and pearly gates to ignite my heart, not throw ice water on it. My heart wanted heaven to be the tuning fork God strikes. I wanted the deepest part of me to vibrate with that ancient yet familiar longing, that desire for something that would fill and overflow my soul.

I was not about to be daunted. There must be positives. If I skirted the glittering celestial city with walls 200 feet thick and made of jasper—just because I didn't like the idea of urban planning in heaven—I'd have nothing to hang my faith on but my imagination. And that could be dangerous.

Slowly the light dawned. The problem lay not with the Bible's descriptions of heavenly glories, but with the way I was looking at those symbols. The Bible was a book to be trusted, so there *must* be more behind the rainbow throne than met the eye.

When it comes to heaven . . . you have to think. When you take time to ponder Scripture, your faith has something to hold onto. Something that's factual and true. Your faith has something to feed on, something from which your dreams about heaven can take root. All this stuff about golden cities and seas of glass had to be clues in some amazing mystery. And if Psalm 25:14 was correct, if "the Lord confides in those who fear him," then it's a mystery that God intends to stimulate me to seek, to rouse and stir my interest until I grasp what heaven is about. When it comes to heaven, there is no limit to what the Lord will confide to those whose faith is rooted in Scripture.

LORD, WHEN I READ the words that describe heaven at face value—gates of pearl, streets of gold—I sometimes feel confused. Let heaven become alive for me. Don't let the negatives turn me off. Help me look beyond the negatives and see the positives. Show me the mysteries of heaven. ✒

WITH EYES OF FAITH

*Now faith is being sure of what we hope
for and certain of what we do not see.*

—*Hebrews 11:1*

If heaven is the home of your spirit, the rest for your soul, the repository of every spiritual investment on earth, then it must grip your heart. And your heart must grip heaven by faith.

Faith means believing in realities that go beyond sense and sight. It is being sure of something you hope for, that is, sure about unfulfilled things in the future. And it's being certain of something you can't see, that is, being aware of unseen divine realities all around you. Faith not only makes you sure that heavenly streets of gold really exist, but it helps you see something beyond the earthly streets of asphalt that exist in the here and now.

Now, it takes no more than a mustard seed-sized grain of faith to be sure of unfulfilled things in the future. It takes no great faith to be aware of unseen divine realities all around us.

Consider Ezekiel. He was just minding his own business by the river when, without warning, God pressed his eyes smack-flat against the brilliance of heaven, a brilliance that the ordinary faithful see from a distance, and then, only through a glass darkly. God revealed to him something supernatural—a whole bunch of unseen divine realities—but God didn't give the prophet a thesaurus of supernatural words. So Ezekiel had to rely on the language of resemblance. The center of the fire looked *like* this, and the faces looked *like* that. In fact, the nearer Ezekiel approaches the burning throne, the less sure his words.

The same is true for the apostle John scrambling to write down his heavenly vision as he sits on the beach on the island of Patmos. Thus, the apostle's best effort to describe what looks like rivers of glass, streets of gold, and gates of pearl.

My point? Were Ezekiel and John sure of what they hoped for? Were they certain of things they had never seen? You bet. They witnessed far into the future something yet to be fulfilled, and when the Lord pulled back the curtain so they could actually see the unseen realities, they trusted Him to bring it to pass.

Ezekiel and John saw their hope. We cannot. And this is why the heavenly song is still an echo. But that's not such a bad thing. When it comes to heaven, if you can move beyond the symbols and be sure of what you hope for, as well as certain that what you do not see is *there*, then you are edging close to the fellowship of prophets and apostles. For although a rainbow throne was emblazoned on their eyes, you can glimpse what the throne symbolizes, and you can see what's beyond.

Onward to the prize before us! Soon his beauty we'll behold;
Soon the pearly gates will open, We shall tread the
    streets of gold.
When we all get to heaven, What a day of rejoicing
    that will be!
When we all see Jesus, We'll sing and shout the victory.
                                        — E.E. Hewitt

HEAVEN IS GOD'S MYSTERY

Trust in the LORD forever, for the LORD,
the LORD, is the Rock eternal.

—Isaiah 26:4

We may strain and squint to see heaven through a glass darkly, but when we, the ordinary faithful, catch a glimpse, we may be in a more blessed state than even that of a prophet. Jesus commends the faith of people like you and me in John 20:29 when He elevates us, saying, "Blessed are those *who have not seen* and yet have believed." Jesus says there is a special kind of blessedness, a unique happiness reserved for people like you and me who dig through earth's dirt to decipher heaven's hieroglyphics.

As weird and strange as the word pictures in the Bible are, they convey one thing for certain: The whole scene in heaven is very real. There's nothing wispy or vaporous about the exact measurements of a twelve-layered foundation of precious stones. It's real, but entirely alien to anything people have heard of on earth.

God has good reasons for describing it this way. If we were able to scale that wall with the ropes and grappling irons of human understanding, then, good grief, our faith wouldn't mean very much.

God designed both heaven and humans so that a cloud of mystery would prevent you and me from fully grasping heaven with language and logic. The apostle Paul, like Ezekiel and John, saw heaven with his own eyes; but unlike them, he was not only unable to describe the sights, he wasn't permitted! The mystery is *supposed* to remain intact. We cannot fashion heaven solely out of the Lincoln Logs of our logic. Even if we could, we would merely be illuminating the sun with a flashlight. We are only allowed to break through the glass darkly by faith.

Heaven is your journey's end, your life's goal, your purpose for going on. You're supposed to be eagerly awaiting it. But trying to grasp heaven without faith is like trying to admire the outside of a huge great cathedral with grand windows. Standing outside, you see an impressive but imposing structure. The building is striking, but has no real glory. But if you go inside the cathedral—which is a little like looking at heaven through eyes of faith—you are breathless as you stand washed in glorious colors from the light that streams through the window.

Faith takes us beyond the imposing and impressive language of golden cities and thrones, and reveals the better, brighter glory inside the walls of the New Jerusalem. Faith takes the descriptions of 24-karat asphalt and big pearls swinging on hinges and makes us certain that what we hope for is far, far better than here.

LORD, I THANK YOU that you have made heaven grander than human language. Help me to grasp heaven by faith. Create within me that certainty that what I am hoping for is far better than what is here on earth. Make heaven come alive for me today.

LOOK BEYOND THE NEGATIVES

You will fill me with joy in your presence, with eternal pleasures at your right hand.

—Psalm 16:11

Do Ezekiel and the writer of Revelation assume that all the other benefits in heaven should outweigh the "no this" and "no that"? No food, no marriage, no moon, no need for good books? Sitting in a wheelchair for decades has loaded me with a lifetime of glorious memories, everything from feeling my fingers on the cool ivory keys of a piano to the euphoria of diving through the breakers at high tide. Such memories flood every nerve and fiber of my being and, thus, my imagination. It's awful to think that the best stuff of which memories are made will have no place in heaven.

But faith tells us these things are inklings of better tastes and enraptured delights yet to come. The whisper of what they are on earth will find complete fulfillment in heaven. *Faith reminds us that every negative is only the reverse side of a fulfilling.* A fulfilling of all that God intended our humanity to be.

There will not be a sun or a moon in heaven. Revelation 21:23 says, "The city does not need the sun or the moon to shine on it." But don't grieve. Heaven won't be less than the wonder you experience over a glorious sunrise or a glowing moonlit night, "for the glory of God gives it light, and the Lamb is its lamp." Even light will have its future divine fulfillment, for it will be a better light. Use your eyes of faith. Think of it in terms of "future divine fulfillments." See that every negative is just a reverse side of a fulfilling.

Faith tells us not to grieve. We will not lose in heaven. We will gain. The Lord who has planted the seed of future divine fulfillments in almost every good thing on earth will carry it on to completion until the day He arrives and makes crystal clear all the unseen divine realities. God won't throw any good thing away.

Heaven has been, and always shall be, a matter of faith. It's not hard to imagine, it's impossible. Absolutely impossible. We have no idea what God is preparing, but heaven promises something far, far better. Cultivate faith that every negative is only the reverse side of a fulfilling. A fulfilling of all that God intended our humanity to be.

LORD, THANK YOU FOR the unseen divine realities all around me. Thank you that heaven will be the fulfilling of all that you intended my life to be. Thank you for helping me look beyond the negatives in the Bible to see that I will not lose anything in heaven. Thank you for the wonders I will gain. Thank you for what you are preparing for me. Thank you for the faith to see every negative as the reverse of a fulfilling. ✐

SEE HEAVEN'S POSITIVE SIDE

*On no day will its gates ever be shut, for
there will be no night there.*

—*Revelation 21:25*

Do you know why a photographer uses a negative to take your photo? He uses it to show us a positive image. It's the same principle when I paint at my easel. Sometimes I choose not to outline a shape, such as a leaf, with a brush, but rather I paint the sky all around the leaf, which then defines its shape. It's called "negative space" painting, and it's a way—some would say a better way—of giving definition to the shapes of leaves against a sky. The artist helps you see by painting what you don't see.

The principle is the same when it comes to heaven: *The negatives are used in order to show us the positive.* On earth, we know all too well what the negatives are: suffering, pain, and death. Show us their opposites, the positive side, and we shall have the best possible idea of the perfect state. For instance, there may be no moon, no marriage, and no need to eat in heaven, as suggested in Revelation 21, but there are also some pretty *good* negatives we can relate to and curiously, they're all listed in Revelation 21 too.

No more sorrow.

No more crying.

No more pain.

No more curse.

And, praise God, no more death.

We'd all admit that the sum of human misery on earth vastly outweighs the sum of human happiness. I can't tell you how much sorrow I've held at bay over the years. Tears could come easily if I allowed myself to think of all the pleasures of movement and sensation I've missed. Diving into a pool and feeling my arms and legs slice through the water. Plucking guitar strings with my fingers. Jogging till my muscles burn. Cracking steam-broiled Maryland crabs with a mallet. Throwing back the covers in the morning and hopping out of bed. Running my hands across my husband's chest and *feeling* it.

Heaven will not be an *unmaking* of all the good things we know, but a new and vastly improved version. Heaven will also be an *undoing* of all the bad things we know as God wipes away every tear and closes the curtain on pain and disappointment.

Are your eyes of faith focusing better? Or rather, can you hear it? The faint echoes of some distant heavenly song? It's whispering words that haven't been spoken since Adam was thrust out of Eden: "There shall be no more sorrow."

> And, Lord, haste the day when the faith shall be sight,
> The clouds be rolled back as a scroll,
> The trump shall resound and the Lord shall
> descend,
> "Even so"—it is well with my soul.
> It is well with my soul.

> —Horatio Spafford

FINDING OUR WAY HOME

*I pray also that the eyes of your heart
may be enlightened in order that you
may know the hope to which he has
called you, the riches of his glorious
inheritance in the saints.*

—*Ephesians 1:18*

Ezekiel is sitting by a river bank when suddenly—in a flash—he squints at the heavens opening above him. "I looked, and I saw . . . an immense cloud with flashing lightning and surrounded by brilliant light. The center of the fire looked like glowing metal, and in the fire was what looked like four living creatures . . . their faces looked like this . . . " Then Ezekiel goes on to describe four heads with eyes, ears, noses, and mouths of oxen and men, lions and eagles.

My heart goes out to Ezekiel. The prophet strained to find words to describe what he witnessed, but after hunting through his dictionary for adequate nouns and adjectives to draw a picture of heaven, he had to fall back on language that was old and familiar.

Heaven is too specific, too real for language. If we've learned anything from the prophet Ezekiel and the apostle John, it's that heaven is real. It's a place—with streets, gates, walls, and rivers.

We are wrong in thinking heaven is wispy, thin, and vaporous. It is earth that is like withering grass, not heaven.

What it takes to know the place Jesus has gone ahead to prepare, is faith. Faith in what God has to say about heaven from His Word. For when God chose to talk about heaven, He did so using the nouns and verbs, syntax and grammar of the Bible. And although He mainly expounded on heaven in highly symbolic books like Ezekiel and Revelation, these symbols are meant to be motivation for our minds and fodder for our faith.

Faith that focuses not *on* scriptural symbols, but *inside* and *beyond* them. Faith that develops the skill of holding onto that heavenly moment. Faith that shows you the way home.

This kind of faith will bring heaven forward into vivid reality. It will bring into vital contact with your heart the things that people call invisible and distant. It will involve your heart and your eyes.

Step back for a moment, focus your eyes of faith, and then walk with me into a world you've heard about from your youth but have never seen: heaven. What will we be like there? What will we do? Where is this place called heaven and why is it called "home"? Look with me through a glass darkly, and you just might discover that Home is closer—and more real—than you ever thought.

> Though I spend my mortal lifetime in this chair,
> I refuse to waste it living in despair. . . .
> For heaven is nearer to me,
> And at times it is all I can see.
> Sweet music I hear
> Coming down to my ear;
> And I know that it's playing for me.
>
> — "Joni's Waltz" by Nancy Honeytree

PART 2

WHO ARE WE IN HEAVEN?

> If I ever reach heaven I expect to find three
> wonders there: first, to meet some I had not
> thought to see there; second, to miss some
> I had expected to see there; and third, the
> greatest wonder of all, to find myself there.
>
> — JOHN NEWTON

I dream about heaven all the time. I can't say my dreams are Techni-
color versions of pearly gates and streets of gold; rather, they're more
like rough sketches or dim reflections.

One extraordinary heaven dream I had one night in a hotel in Stavanger, Norway. As the cold Norwegian wind rattled my bedroom window, I snuggled down and slipped into the most amazing dream.

I saw myself standing in a bright yellow bathing suit at the edge of a pool. I stretched my arms above my head, arched my back, and gracefully dove into the water. When I came up and slicked my hair with my hands, I was stunned to see them glow, all rose-red wet and honey-ivory, bathed in life, beauty, and well-being. I pressed my palms to my nose. They smelled wild and sweet.

I cocked my head and admired my outstretched arms and then looked around. You know how we say "the water sparkles"? In my dream it was doing exactly that. The air was sparkling too. Everything was flashing, clear, and golden.

I saw a friend sitting poolside, relaxing in a chair under a white cabana and watching me. He was my old friend but a thousand times more himself, and when our eyes met, youth infused my heart. I smiled, waved, and then began swimming, smoothly parting the water with long, powerful strokes. After a while, my friend dove in. There was no need to talk; our smiles said that we were friends for the first time again. We swam together stroke-for-stroke. And the longer we swam, the stronger we grew.

It was the most remarkable dream I've ever had. When I woke up, I had no doubt it was a dream about heaven. I saw it with the eyes of my heart.

One day the dream will come true.

One day no more bulging middles or balding tops. Just a quick leapfrog over the tombstone and it's the body you've always dreamed of. Fit and trim, smooth and sleek. It makes me want to break up into giggles right now!

Dream with me. . . .

New Bodies

The Lord Jesus Christ, who, by the power that enables him to bring everything under his control, will transform our lowly bodies so that they will be like his glorious body.

—*Philippians 3:20b-21*

Our lowly bodies will be like his glorious body. A promise like this almost raises more questions than answers. Will we recognize each other? Will my husband be "Ken Tada" and my mother, "Margaret Johanna Eareckson"?

Another thing. What about people who died centuries before? Will God vacuum up the winds, collect and sort everyone's body particles, and divvy out the correct DNA?

These questions became real to me in the summer of 1990 when my ninety-year-old father passed away. He had led a cowboy roughrider life. So it was not unusual that summer for my family and Ken and me to drive to the top of Pikes Peak to scatter my father's ashes.

We found a private place near the edge of a cliff. Thousands of feet beneath us spread a green valley patchworked in sun and cloud shadows. An eagle hang glided above our heads. My mother stepped closer to the edge, took her husband's ashes in her hand, and threw them to the wind. I watched with wet eyes as a gust carried my father's ashes up and beyond the clouds.

Billions and billions of people have lived on earth and have probably shared the same dust and ashes. It seems silly, but how will John Eareckson's molecules remain distinct from the rest?

The apostle Paul cuts those big scary questions down to size when he says, "When you sow, you do not plant the body that will be, but just a seed, perhaps of wheat or of something else. But God gives it a body as he has determined, and to each kind of seed he gives its own body" (1 Corinthians 15:37-38).

Trying to understand what our bodies will be like in heaven is much like expecting an acorn to understand his destiny of roots, bark, branches, and leaves. Or asking a caterpillar to appreciate flying. Or a peach pit to fathom being fragrant. Or a coconut to grasp what it means to sway in the ocean breeze. Our eternal bodies will be so grand, so glorious, that we can only catch a fleeting glimpse of the splendor to come.

It's no wonder you and I get stymied thinking about our resurrection bodies. We may not be able to describe the changes, but we know it's the same *"it."* You and what you will one day be are one and the same—yet different.

Our lowly bodies will be like his glorious body. Astounding.

LORD, MY POINT OF view seems so limited when I try to envision what it will be like to have a new body. Will I look different from the angels? Will I be able to eat, sleep, run and play like I do here on earth? Help expand my limited vision. Grant me a joyful trust in knowing that you will work out all the details.

How Are the Dead Raised?

But someone may ask, "How are the dead raised? With what kind of body will they come?" How foolish! What you sow does not come to life unless it dies.

—*1 Corinthians 15:35-36*

Have you ever seen those nature specials on public television? The ones where they put the camera up against a glass to show a dry, old lima bean in the soil? Through time-lapse photography, you watch it shrivel, turn brown, and die. Then, miraculously, the dead shell of that little bean splits open and a tiny lima leg-like root sprouts out. The old bean is shoved aside against the dirt as the little green plant swells.

But one thing is for sure: it's a lima bean plant. There's no mistaking it for anything other than what it is. It has absolute identity. Positively, plain as day, a lima bean plant. It may come out of the earth different than when it went in, but it's the same.

So it is with the resurrection body. We'll have absolute identification with our body that died. The "daddy" I meet in heaven will be my dad; he won't be neutered in my eyes, stripped of all the trappings that made him my father. He may come forth from the earth different than when he was buried, but he won't be mistaken for anyone else.

And what about his dust and ashes scattered to the winds? How many of my father's molecules are required to be reassembled before he can be raised? Very little, I suspect.

Besides, how much of that old lima bean was the "seed" out of which life miraculously came forth? The best botanists in the world can't answer that one. No one knows how much of that seed is required or even how life can spring from a dead seed. It's one of God's miracles of nature.

So it will be with the resurrection. God will not have to use every part of your body in order to resurrect it. Anyway, you do not possess today any particle of your body that you had a few years ago. We learn in Biology 101 that human cells are being replaced every three and one-half years. The flesh and blood that make up "you" today is not the same flesh and blood you had in your teens. Yet, somehow, the particular person that you are carries on.

Jesus gives a simple biology lesson in John 12:24: "I tell you the truth, unless a kernel of wheat falls to the ground and dies, it remains only a single seed. But if it dies, it produces many seeds." It is no more difficult to believe in the resurrection than it is to believe in the harvest.

LORD, I THANK YOU for the promise of resurrection. I thank you that you have placed within my earthly body the seed for my spiritual body in heaven. Grant me a freedom from the fear of dying and replace it with a joy of reuniting with loved ones in our home in heaven.

WHAT KIND OF BODY
WILL WE HAVE?

When you sow, you do not plant the body that will be, but just a seed, perhaps of wheat or of something else. But God gives it a body as he has determined, and to each kind of seed he gives its own body.

—*1 Corinthians 15:37-38*

You *do not plant the body that will be.* I learned this lesson on one of those blustery November afternoons when I tend to get thoughtful and meditative. I glanced outside my window and spied a fat, furry squirrel doing his autumn ritual of collecting acorns. I watched him sniff each one, inspecting them in his paws, then stuffing his cheeks with the tastiest nuts. Others he dropped on the ground.

The acorns he discarded rolled around in the stiff breeze. I knew most of them would blow away. Others would remain on the dirt to dry in the chilly air. And a few, just a few, would take root under the soil. They would be the ones next season to sprout forth green shoots of new life. These were the acorns destined to be trees.

I shook my head in amazement. If you were to tell that tiny acorn that one day he would be as tall as a building with heavy branches and thick, green leaves, a tree so great it would house many squirrels, that nut would say you were crazy. A gigantic oak tree bears absolutely no resemblance to an acorn. The two, although related, seem as different as night and day. Somehow, somewhere within that acorn is the promise and pattern of the tree it will become.

Somehow, somewhere within you is the pattern of the heavenly person you will become, and if you want to catch a glimpse of how glorious and full of splendor your body will be, just do a comparison. Compare a hairy peach pit with the tree it becomes, loaded with fragrant blossoms and sweet fruit. They are totally different, yet the same.

Somewhere in my broken, paralyzed body is the seed of what I shall become. The paralysis makes what I am to become all the more grand when you contrast atrophied, useless legs against splendorous resurrected legs. There's no way I can comprehend it all because I'm just an "acorn" when it comes to understanding heaven.

But I'll tell you this: Whether flinging a Frisbee or flying past Ursa Major. Scaling walls or walking through them. Speaking with friends or conversing with angels. Whether trout fishing in the Crystal Sea or going for seconds at the Wedding Supper, at all times and in all places we shall be perfectly fitted for our environment, whether it be the new heavens or new earth. Whatever my little acorn shape becomes, in all its power and honor, I'm ready for it!

> When I shall reach the more excellent glory,
> And all my trials are passed,
> I shall be like Him, O wonderful story!
> I shall be like Him at last.
>
> — W. A. Spencer

THE QUESTIONS WE ASK

*And just as we have borne the likeness of
the earthly man [Adam], so shall we
bear the likeness of the man from heaven
[Jesus].*

—*1 Corinthians 15:49*

How are the dead raised? With what kind of body will they come?
Not even a Ph.D. in Botany can explain how life comes out of
death, even in something so simple as a seed. The apostle Paul cuts
our big scary questions about death down to size when he says in
1 Corinthians 15:35, "Guys, get real. Open your eyes." And start-
ing with verse 36, he sketches a few lessons from nature, "What
you sow does not come to life unless it dies. When you sow, you
do not plant the body that will be, but just a seed, perhaps of wheat
or of something else. But God gives it a body as he has determined,
and to each kind of seed he gives its own body."

True to the apostle Paul and his lessons from nature, all we
have to do is open our eyes and look around. Compare a caterpillar with a butterfly. A wet, musty flower bulb with an aro-
matic hyacinth. A hairy coconut with a graceful palm tree.

"You do not plant the body that will be, but just a seed. . . .
The body that is sown is perishable, it is raised imperishable; it

is sown in dishonor, it is raised in glory; it is sown in weakness, it is raised in power; it is sown a natural body, it is raised a spiritual body." *It* is sown, *it* is raised. We may not be able to describe the changes, but we know it's the same *"it."*

Peach pits. Acorns and oak trees. Examples in nature are what the Bible invites us to use since "what we will be has not yet been made known" (1 John 3:2). One of the best ways to understand the resurrection is to take a field trip after the apostle Paul's lesson in nature: Go find an acorn on the ground, look up into the billowy skirts of the tree from which it fell, and then praise God that "so it will be with the resurrection of the dead."

I'm ready to have this lowly body transformed. That means I won't merely be revived from the dead, like Lazarus when he came out of his tomb. People who return from the dead— whether from the tomb or off the operating table—aren't, like Christ, able then to appear and disappear, walk through walls, or transport themselves through time and space with a single thought.

No, I will bear the likeness of Jesus, the man from heaven. Like His, mine will be an actual, literal body perfectly suited for earth *and* heaven

Are you dreaming about heaven?

I'm ready for it.

LORD, MY QUESTIONS SEEM so scary when I view them from this side of eternity. Give me glorified eyes to see the hidden potential in your promises about heaven. Transform me even now to your likeness a little more each day. ✐

A NEW HEART

*Create in me a pure heart, O God, and
renew a steadfast spirit within me.*

—*Psalm 51:10*

However much I relish the idea of leaving this wheelchair behind, that is still, for me, not the best part of heaven.

I can put up with legs and arms that don't obey. Hands that refuse to pick up things no matter how much my mind commands them to move are a fact of life. I can cope with this.

However, there's something with which I can't cope. And the closer to heaven I draw, the less I'm able to adjust to it. I am sick and tired of "when I want to do good, evil is right there with me. For in my inner being I delight in God's law; but I see another law at work in the members of my body, waging war against the law of my mind and making me a prisoner of the law of sin at work within my members" (Romans 7:21–24).

It pains me to keep erring and straying, to do things that I shouldn't do, to always fall face-flat in the dirt, grieving that I miserably offend the God I love. My heart is soiled and stained, and that drives me to the Lord on my knees (at least, metaphorically). What's odd is, the closer I draw to Jesus, the more intense the heat of the battle.

Never do I feel more on the front-line of this battle than when I offer praise to God. Right in the middle of adoring Him in prayer or singing a praise hymn, my heart will start wandering off into some wicked thought. I have to grab my heart by the aorta and jerk it in line time and again!

That's why the best part of heaven will be a completely purified heart.

One day Jesus will come back to complete the salvation He began when I first believed. At this present time, the spirit is willing but the flesh is weak. The day is coming, however, when instead of being a hindrance to the spirit, the body will be the perfect vessel for the expression of my glorified mind, will, and emotions.

True, it will be wonderful to stand, stretch, and reach to the sky, but it will be more wonderful to offer praise that is pure. I won't be crippled by distractions. Disabled by insincerity. I won't be handicapped by a ho-hum halfheartedness. My heart will join with yours and bubble over with effervescent adoration. We will finally be able to fellowship fully with the Father and the Son.

For me, this will be the best part of heaven.

OH, LORD JESUS! Thank you for the good news in your Word that my body will be redeemed. Thank you that you will remove all traces of sin from my heart and replace it with sincere adoration. Clothe my heart in righteousness even now and accept my feeble praise for your everlasting love. ✎

A NEW MIND

*Now we see but a poor reflection as in a
mirror; then we shall see face to face.
Now I know in part; then I shall know
fully, even as I am fully known.*

—*1 Corinthians 13:12*

I look forward to heaven because I've got a lot invested there. A
new body. A new heart free of sin. But I have some other friends
who have just as much, if not more, invested.

I encountered these friends in a Sunday school class not long
ago where I shared my testimony. They were young adults with
mental handicaps, some from Down's syndrome, others with
autism or various brain injuries. The teacher clapped her hands
and directed the class's attention my way.

One or two of them leaned on their elbows and studied me
in my wheelchair with casual curiosity. I caught their interest
when I flailed my useless arms and told them that the guys that
run Six Flags Over Magic Mountain wouldn't let me ride the
giant water slide. They felt bad. Some booed. Then I told them
that one day, when I get my new body, I'd not only master the
water slide, but also snow ski the Cornice at Mammoth Mountain or run the New York City marathon if I wanted to.

"It's going to be great having a new body." I smiled at the men and women who were now looking with intense interest. Everybody wanted to hear about heaven.

I challenged them to come up with other neat things I'd do with a new body. They thought it would be great for me to walk into McDonald's and stand in line. I'd be able to unwrap a Snicker's bar. I could flush a toilet.

The class wanted to talk more about heaven. They invented all sorts of wild and wonderful heavenly activities. Riding giraffes. Going on a picnic with Jesus. Petting sharks.

As their enthusiasm mounted, I finally blurted, "Hey guys, I may have a new body, but one day, you will have new *minds!*" Amidst whistles and cheers, I went on to say, "You will think high-powered, super-charged thoughts and know just about everything there is to know. Your brain will burn rubber! Most of all, you and Jesus will be together, and you'll have lots of things to talk about."

By the time Sunday school was over, the class was well on their way to setting their hearts and minds on heavenly glories above. I thought I had taught them a lesson about heaven, but they had taught me what it meant to "have the mind of Christ." No need to worry about feeling dumb or not knowing the answers. "We will know as we are known." A new mind! Oh, happy day, we shall have the mind of Christ!

LORD, I CAN'T WAIT until I get to heaven and have my mind made perfect. No more imperfect thoughts. No more sad memories. No more ignorance. My redeemed body will have a redeemed mind. Grant me a foretaste of that perfect mind as you mirror your thoughts in me today. ✒

THOUGHTS AND MEMORIES

*Behold, I will create new heavens and a new
earth. The former things will not be remembered, nor will they come to mind. But be
glad and rejoice forever in what I will create.*

—Isaiah 65:17

One day, you will have a new mind! And the shine of our best
thoughts and memories will be made more resplendent as they
are magnified through our new mind.

But what about the sad thoughts left over from earth? Are
bad things excluded?

Bad things will not, as Isaiah observes, come to mind, for
they will be blocked out by the brilliance of the knowledge of
God. Our ignorance or imperfect thoughts and memories won't
be erased so much as eclipsed, like the stars are mitigated by the
rising of the sun. Something so dazzling is going to happen in the
world's finale that its light will obscure every dark memory. We
won't forget so much as have no need nor desire to remember.

Think of perfect obedience to the Ten Commandments. Having no other gods before the Lord? Easy, we will be one with Him.

Jealousy? You and I will have nothing but admiration for
whomever is selected to sit on the right and left hand of Christ.

Keeping the Sabbath? We will have entered God's . . . Sabbath-rest of peace and joy for eternity.

Adultery? I will love everyone as perfectly as Christ loves. I will find in every person that facet of the Lord's loveliness that only he or she can uniquely reflect—I'm going to be in love with a mountain of people, both men and women!

Coveting? We will be joint-heirs with Christ. We'll have everything.

Bearing false witness? The father of lies will be dead. Only truth will spring from our heart.

Misusing the name of the Lord? Only praise will be on our lips.

And with the mind of Christ we shall "know fully." While we were on earth, . . . we scratched our heads and wondered how the matted mesh of threads in Romans 8:28 could possibly be woven together for our good.

On earth, the underside of the tapestry was tangled and unclear; but in heaven, we will stand amazed to see the topside of the tapestry and how God beautifully embroidered each circumstance into a pattern for our good and His glory. This will be one of those fringe benefits not essential for our eternal happiness, but simply nice to know. We will see that nothing—absolutely nothing—was wasted and that every tear counted and every cry was heard.

Oh, happy day, we shall have the mind of Christ!

> May the mind of Christ, my Savior,
> Live in me from day to day,
> By His love and power controlling
> All I do and say.

> — Kate B. Wilkinson

A PERFECT BODY AND SOUL

*Be perfect, therefore, as your heavenly
Father is perfect.*

—*Matthew 5:48*

Perfection of body and soul can, to some, sound boring.
I have two friends, John and Mike, with whom perfection just
doesn't click. They are wonderful brothers in Christ, but they
are the robust sort. The idea of a "never-ending relationship at
the feet of Jesus," though comforting, doesn't get them charged.

Perfection? Nah, they savor the spice of a good argument
now and then. "Who wants a friend, or even a wife, who always
agrees with you?" they say.

These guys would rather help pave the streets of gold with
titanium monster trucks, back loaders, and steamrollers. They'll
take kayaking on the River of Life any day, and would rather
take Joseph and Daniel fly-fishing than sit around and listen to
them explain dream therapy.

I'm not about to fault these friends of mine. Frankly, I hope
they take me fly-fishing as well. They're just being left-brained.
They're into logic and explanations.

Perfection of body and soul has nothing to do with casting the
perfect fly or playing the perfect round of golf. We've got to watch

it. We can't construct heaven with the Lincoln Logs of our logic. What we imagine turns clunky when we rely on earthly images.

We have to begin to get our hearts and minds somewhat in tune for heaven. You have to spend time doing the "be ye perfect as I am perfect" thing here on earth before you can enjoy the idea of heavenly perfection. Heaven is a prepared place for prepared people. Otherwise, heaven is a turnoff.

To John and Mike this, at first, may chill rather than awaken their desire for heaven. But whether left-brained or right-brained, whether macho or meditative, the closer we draw to the Lord Jesus and the more we set our hearts and minds on heavenly glories above, the better prepared we shall be for heaven's perfection. Fellowship won't mean sitting at the feet of Jesus and fighting back boredom while everyone else is enraptured. No. Fellowship will be the best of what earthly friendship merely hinted at.

I would like to tell John and Mike, "Hey, don't forget, Christ knows better than you what it means to be human. He sailed on the seas, hiked mountains, and slept under the stars by a rushing brook. He realizes what gets your heart pumping. Remember, He made you. You won't stop being human. Rather, you'll enjoy the full richness of all that your humanity was designed to be. You, with all your propensity for chumming it up around the campfire, will be a better you!"

And a better you is a perfect you.

LORD, I HAVE TO admit the thought of a perfect body and soul sounds boring to me sometimes. No goals to reach for. No challenge. Perfection is just too . . . perfect. Take my spirit and work in me. Begin to live your perfect life through me, one day at a time. Prepare me for heaven, regardless of the cost. Make me more like you. ✐

A PARTY WITH FRIENDS!

> *Then the angel said to me, "Write: 'Blessed are those who are invited to the wedding supper of the Lamb!'" And he added, "These are the true words of God."*
>
> —*Revelation 19:9*

Heaven's Wedding Supper of the Lamb will be the perfect party. The Father has been sending out invitations and people have been RSVP-ing through the ages. Jesus has gone ahead to hang the streamers, prepare the feast, and make our mansion ready. And like any party, what will make it sweet is the fellowship—fellowship with our glorious Savior and with our friends and family.

One person I'm particularly eager to see in heaven is . . . my friend, Steve Estes. Next to my husband, he's my dearest friend. Even though we only visit occasionally over the phone, our friendship remains strong and secure. We shall be forever friends.

Our friendship is no coincidence. How do I know? In Acts 17:26 it says, "From one man he made every nation of men, that they should inhabit the whole earth; and *he determined the times set for them and the exact places where they should live.*"

Did you catch that? A few more miles between our houses, or a few more years between our ages, and chances are, we would never have encountered each other.

This has powerful implications for eternity. Friendship initiated on earth barely has time to get started; we only scratch its surface in the few short years we reside on earth. Its greater and richer dimension will unfold in heaven.

How it will pan out is yet to be seen, but this I know: All the earthly things we enjoy with our friends here will find their more exalted expression in heaven. It'll be a place where we *do* things with our friends for the sheer joy of being together and blessed by God.

And, oh, the things we shall do! Together, friends will eat the fruit of the tree of life and be pillars in the temple of God. Together, we shall receive the morning star and be crowned with life, righteousness, and glory. Most of all, together we shall fall on our faces at the foot of the throne and worship our Savior forever.

Dreaming about this makes missing dear friends more bearable. It even makes my relationship with friends who have died and gone on to glory sweet and close.

The same is true for you. These dear ones in your life are no coincidence. You could have been born in another time and another place, but God determined to "people" your life with these particular friends. These special ones strike a resonant chord in your heart. In friendship, God opens your eyes to the glories of Himself.

FATHER, WHAT A WONDERFUL thought it is to realize that you have set the times and places in my life in such a way that I could be friends with these treasured ones. Thank you for my friends. And thank you for letting our paths cross. They have been your light to me in so many ways.

To Bow in Worship

*Come let us bow down and worship, let
us kneel before the Lord our Maker.*

—*Psalm 95:6*

I grew up in a little Reformed Episcopal Church where they preached the gospel, read the liturgy, sang hymns from the heart, and kneeled in prayer. Banners and candles, processionals and recessionals were a part of regular worship. Sunday morning worship was serious business, and I learned as a child what it meant to bend my knee before the Lord. Yes, kneeling felt hard on the knees, but what it did for my heart felt better.

Once at a convention, the speaker closed his message by asking everyone in the large room to push their chairs away from the tables and, if they were able, to kneel on the carpeted floor for prayer. I watched as everyone in the room—maybe five or six hundred people—hiked up their cuffs and got down on their knees. I couldn't stop the tears.

I wasn't crying out of pity or because I felt awkward or different. Tears were streaming because I was struck with the beauty of seeing so many people on bended knees before the Lord. It was a picture of heaven.

I don't intend to make an issue of kneeling. God listens when His people pray standing, sitting, lying prone or prostrate.

What's my point about kneeling? It's just that I wish I could do it. It's impossible for me to bow in worship.

Sitting there, I was reminded that in heaven I will be free to jump up, dance, kick, and do aerobics. And although I'm sure Jesus will be delighted to watch me rise on tiptoe, there's something I plan to do that may please Him more. If possible, somewhere, sometime before the party gets going, sometime before the guests are called to the banquet table at the Wedding Feast of the Lamb, the first thing I plan to do on resurrected legs is to drop on grateful, glorified knees. I will quietly kneel at the feet of Jesus.

To *not* move will be my chance to demonstrate heartfelt thanks to the Lord for the grace He dispensed year after year when my legs and hands were limp and motionless. To not move will be my last chance to present a sacrifice of praise—paralyzed praise.

The day is drawing near when I'll be able to kneel again. I know it, I can feel it. Heaven is just around the corner. So, do me a favor: Do what so many of us who are paralyzed or too lame or old *can't* do. Flip open your Bible to Psalm 95:6; read it aloud and take its advice. And when you kneel in prayer, be grateful for knees that bend to the will of God. Be grateful you're destined for heaven, for a new heart, mind, and body.

> But now we wait . . . wait . . .
> wait for our Risen Lord
> who will reward we who weep
> yet still seek Him above all
> so . . .
> stand we tall together
> for the first time ever
> then fall, please, on grateful knees . . .
> Eternity is ours.

—Joni Tada

PART 3

WHAT WILL WE DO IN HEAVEN?

> The joys of heaven are not the joys of
> passive contemplation, of dreamy
> remembrance, of perfect repose; but
> they are described thus, . . . "His ser-
> vants serve him and see his face."
>
> — ALEXANDER MACLAREN

It's easy for me to "be joyful in hope," as it says in Romans 12:12, and
that's exactly what I've been doing for the past twenty-odd years. I, with
shriveled, bent fingers, atrophied muscles, gnarled knees, and no feeling

from the shoulders down, will one day have a new body, light, bright, and clothed in righteousness—powerful and dazzling. No other religion, no other philosophy promises new bodies, hearts, and minds. Only in the Gospel of Christ do hurting people find such incredible hope.

Heaven is by no means ambiguous. Isaiah 65:17 says that God is planning "new heavens and a new earth." Did you get that? A new earth with earthy things in it. Nothing clunky . . . no gawky images . . . just warm and wonderful things that make earth . . . earth. If there are streets, rivers, trees, and mountains in the new earth, like the Bible says there will be, then why not all the other good things? Why not . . . rocking chairs?

Again, underline that word "earth." It just wouldn't be "earth" without animals. Horses in heaven? Yes. I think animals are some of God's best and most avant-garde ideas; why would He throw out His greatest creative achievements? I'm not talking about my pet schnauzer, Scrappy, dying and going to heaven. I'm talking about new animals fit for a new order of things. Isaiah foresaw lions and lambs lying down together, as well as bears, cows, and cobras; and John foresaw the saints galloping on white horses. I have no idea where they will fit, but I'm certain they will populate part of the new heavens and new earth.

[And] there are countless people I'm waiting to see. Queen Esther, Daniel, Jonah, and, of course, Mary and Martha. If the disciples were able to recognize Elijah and Moses standing next to Jesus on the Mount of Transfiguration—saints they had never laid eyes on—then the same is true for us. I can't wait to meet them all!

I'm convinced these things will really happen. It will be the answer to all our longings.

And not only our longings, but those of Jesus.

REWARDS IN HEAVEN

Now there is in store for me the crown of righteousness, which the Lord, the righteous Judge, will award to me on that day— and not only to me, but also to all who have longed for his appearing.

—2 Timothy 4:8

Somewhere in the midst of the royal heavenly celebration—maybe right before the banquet or soon after—Jesus will rise, ascend His throne, and present rewards and crowns to all the guests. This is a *most* unusual celebration. For it is not the guests who come bearing gifts, but the Host. The Lord Jesus does all the gift giving.

And these rewards aren't your average party favors. We shall be given crowns.

Maybe some adults pooh-pooh the idea of rewards, but I don't. The child in me jumps up and down to think God might actually award me something. I remember when I took piano lessons as a kid and would squirm with delight on my bench whenever Mrs. Merson pasted gold crowns on my sheet music for a job well done. I wasn't so much overjoyed with my performance as I was in pleasing Mrs. Merson. My focus wasn't on what I did; it was on her approval. Sophisticated adults aren't into such whimsy, but children sure are. So, for all the children whom Jesus said were best fit for the kingdom of heaven, get ready for God to show you not only His pleasure, but His approval.

What does a crown in heaven look like? Psalm 149:4 gives a hint as to what kind of crown God means, "For the Lord takes delight in his people; he crowns the humble with salvation." Aha! God probably doesn't mean a literal crown, because salvation isn't something you put on your head. Heavenly crowns must represent something He does, something He gives, as when He crowns us with salvation. Anyway, this is more resplendent and illustrious than any old hunk of platinum with a lot of sparkly things in it.

There's also the *crown of life* in James 1:12, reserved for those who persevere under trials. This means God awards us with life eternal.

There's the *crown of rejoicing* in 1 Thessalonians 2:19, given to believers who introduce others to Christ. This means God awards us with joy that lasts forever.

The *incorruptible crown* in 1 Corinthians 9:25, presented to those who are found pure and blameless on the judgment day. Nothing God gives will ever perish, spoil, or fade.

And in 1 Peter 5:2-4, there's the *crown of glory*, reserved for Christian leaders who have guided others. God awards us glory that will never diminish, but only increase.

And my favorite, the *crown of righteousness* mentioned in 2 Timothy 4:8 for those who are itching to have Jesus come back. God will award us right-standing with Him that never changes.

LORD JESUS, THE CHILD in me truly jumps up and down when I realize you have a reward in heaven set aside for me. I thank you for the knowledge that I give you pleasure when I follow your ways. Find me faithful to you as I anxiously await your return. ✐

PRAISE FROM GOD

Therefore judge nothing before the appointed time; wait till the Lord comes. He will bring to light what is hidden in darkness and will expose the motives of men's hearts. At that time each will receive his praise from God.

—*1 Corinthians 4:5*

I never could understand why Christians longed to go to heaven. To me, heaven was a place where not only God would know all and see all, but my friends and family would too. I pictured myself . . . passing people I respected, like my ninth-grade teacher, my hockey coach, and my Sunday school leader. I spotted others like the handicapped boy in school I made fun of and the girl down the street I beat up in a fistfight. I pictured . . . sinking into a seat, and cringing as God then rolled the movie of my life for all to gawk at. Talk about guilt and judgment!

I'm inclined to believe that the real judgment seat of Christ will be quite different.

Just consider 1 Corinthians 4:5: "Therefore judge nothing before the appointed time; wait till the Lord comes. He will bring to light what is hidden in darkness and will expose the motives of men's hearts. At that time each will receive his praise from God."

Read that one more time. *Each will receive his praise from God.* When Christ ascends His throne and sits at the judgment seat, I don't believe He'll roll an uncut, uncensored version of your life. He won't wear the scowl of a rigid and inflexible judge who bangs the gavel and reads aloud your sins for the court record. No, that already happened at another judgment. The judgment at the cross. It was there the Father slammed down the gavel and pronounced His Son "Guilty!" as He became sin for us. It went on record in the courts of heaven and then the indictment was canceled with the words "Paid in Full," written not with red ink, but red blood.

Your sins will not condemn you in heaven. Psalm 103:10–12 promises that: "He does not treat us as our sins deserve or repay us according to our iniquities. For as high as the heavens are above the earth, so great is his love for those who fear him; as far as the east is from the west, so far has he removed our transgressions from us." If you have placed your trust in Christ for having borne your transgressions on His cross, then you have nothing to fear. He did away with it. Erased it. Sin no longer has power to wound or to inflict remorse and regret.

No one will be left out. Each will receive his reward.

> **FATHER, YOUR PROMISE THAT** my sins will not condemn me in heaven is awe-inspiring. The fact that I will have nothing to fear at the day of judgment is reassuring. The knowledge that I should receive praise from you, the Creator of the universe, is mind boggling. But that your son bears my punishment is truly humbling. As I bow before you, may my lips and my thoughts resound your praise, today and always. ✐

THE JUDGMENT SEAT OF CHRIST

*Each one should be careful how he builds.
For no one can lay any foundation other
than the one already laid, which is Jesus
Christ. If any man builds on this foundation
using gold, silver, costly stones, wood, hay, or
straw—his work will be shown for what it is.*

—1 Corinthians 3:10b–13a

The judgment seat of Christ is not a trial to determine whether you are guilty or innocent. I like to picture a judge's stand at a housing contractor's convention where rewards are distributed to all the architects, builders, foremen, and construction crews. The judge examines the quality of each man's work. Each receives praise for what he has built and how he has built it. And the prize? The judge will say, "Well done! You've accomplished much with these few buildings, now we will put you in charge of a big development." Thus, the architects and foremen are awarded larger and more elaborate contracts. And the builders get to roll up their sleeves and tackle the newest and best homes on the market. Each person walks away from the convention happy, heartened, and with an increased capacity to serve.

It's a little like this for Christians. Every day we have the opportunity to roll up our spiritual sleeves and apply our spiritual energies toward building something that lasts, in our lives and the lives of others. We are warned to be careful and choose as our building materials gold, silver, and costly stones; that is, service rendered out of a pure heart, a right motive, and an eye for God's glory. Or we can choose wood, hay, or straw; things done out of an impure motive and an eye to our own glory.

One look from the Lord will scrutinize the quality of what we've built, and selfish service will be consumed in a fiery flash. Burnt away will be those times I gave the gospel out of puffed-up pride. Up in flames will go any service I performed for "performance's sake." Reduced to charcoal will be manipulative behavior and lies-dressed-up-like-truth.

One look from the Lord will consume worthless service. But it will illuminate God-honoring service. Like gold and precious stones, pure service will easily survive the test. It is *this* for which we shall be commended. "Well done, good and faithful servant! You have been faithful with a few things; I will put you in charge of many things. Come and share your master's happiness!" (Matthew 25:23).

I WANT TO PUT to death every selfish motive and prideful pretense so that when the Lord's eyes scan my service, what I have built will stand the test. I want to be careful how I build, and realize that every smile, prayer, or ounce of muscle or money sacrificed is a golden girder, brick, or two-by-four. I want everything I do here to be an eternal investment, a way of building something bright and beautiful there. I'm constructing with an eye toward eternity, and so can you. ✒

ETERNAL, LOVING WORSHIP

Sing to him, sing praise to him; tell of all his wonderful acts. Glory in his holy name; let the hearts of those who seek the LORD rejoice.

—Psalm 105:2-3

I can just see my two macho friends, John and Mike, in heaven, sons of God in the fullest sense. I picture them grabbing each other, jumping up and down, and exclaiming, "Oh boy, now we get to *do* something!" They rub their hands together, roll up the sleeves on their white robes, and ask, "Okay, Lord, what are our jobs? We're ready to go!"

Our most important service to God in heaven is worship. Our first assignment is praise. Heaven is a place of eternal, loving worship. Our service will be to continually praise God without interruption.

"Huh?" I can just see my guy friends say.

They might dare think, *Isn't this going to get a little tedious after a while?*

You could only say this if you conceive of truth, goodness, or even eternity and heaven as static and abstract. It's not. Not static, but dynamic. Not abstract, but concrete.

In heaven, praise won't be inert and abstract, like the impression you have when you hear a musty old hymn sung by a handful of stone-faced worshipers in a huge cathedral. Or like the feeling you get when singing a praise chorus for the hundredth time. Our heart really doesn't care if the song itself is new—some of the oldest hymns of the church are still fresh—but our heart cannot tolerate words or songs of praise that have dug ruts over the passage of time. If joy and satisfaction aren't in your worship, then you know you're missing the mark. You want to offer something fresh that hits home in the heart of God.

In heaven, praise will never be empty or short of its target. Worship won't be suspended between us at point A and God at point B. This kind of praise may be endured on earth, but it's hanging in the breeze when it comes to heaven.

Praise in heaven will have substance. Everything in heaven will have more substance than we ever dreamed.

In eternal praise, the thrill of getting there will be more than matched by what we see, hold, taste, and wear when we arrive. For John and Mike, the thrill will include not only climbing the mountain, but enjoying the view from the top, and doing both at the same time. We shall travel hopefully and arrive, as it were, all at the same moment—we will no longer desire our God who is absent, but rejoice in our God who is present.

> **LORD, EVEN THOUGH I** have had some wonderful worship experiences here on earth I can't wait for the dynamic worship we will share together around your throne in heaven. Help me to get ready for heavenly worship by cultivating fresh new ways to praise you now.

PRAISING HIM FOREVER

*Those who are wise will shine like the
brightness of the heavens, and those who
lead many to righteousness, like the stars
for ever and ever.*

—Daniel 12:3

Our worship of God will never end. It's like the excitement I
used to feel as a child when my father would read me a story. To
me, the beginning was always the most fascinating part. It was
fresh. That's because the beginning touches something timeless
that no events in time can tarnish. Unfortunately, as the story
progressed, my interest frittered away, along with my wonder.

Just as in a story, people labor through chapter after chapter
of their lives, and the fascination and wonder fade as the years go
by in a succession of events. We grow tired and weary, never able
to grasp the dreams that enthralled us at the beginning. The state
that we long for is never quite embodied. And so, our interest
fritters away.

But for Christians, all the things that stir our interest about
eternity *will be embodied*. Like a grand story, it will always be an
enchanting beginning. Or better yet, the end *and* the beginning,

as God is both Alpha and Omega, the First and the Last, the Beginning and the End.

Little wonder flesh and blood cannot inherit heaven. To be at both the beginning and the end, or to wear righteousness like a bright raiment, requires a complete metamorphosis. Our earthly bodies would never be able to contain the joy or express the praise. Our fleshly hearts and minds could never hold it all. Heavenly worship would split the seams and break the human container. We little caterpillars and peach pits need to go from death to life so that our glorified bodies and hearts are fit for the filling and overflowing of ecstatic praise.

Praise will not be something we will be assigned or commanded to do; it will be natural. In heaven, we, like diamonds, will give off prism-like praise as every facet of our being reflects His Shekinah glory. The crowning glory for us will be in losing ourselves and yet finding ourselves in the Alpha and the Omega. A supernatural effervescent response of the born-again creature, new and fit for heaven. It will be impossible not to praise Him.

Who can find words for such worship? What thesaurus has the nouns or adjectives to convey "eating" life like fruit from a tree or "tasting" the Bread of Heaven? I want to lift up my hands and whisper, "Oh, the depth of the riches of the wisdom and knowledge of God! How unsearchable his judgments, and his paths beyond tracing out! . . . For from him and through him and to him are all things. To him be the glory forever! Amen" (Romans 11:33, 36).

Heaven is a place full of glory, light, and praise. I can't wait!

LORD, CREATE IN ME a new sense of beginnings without endings. Preoccupy my thoughts with your praise beginning today. ✒

SERVING GOD IN HEAVEN

"Well done, my good servant!" his master replied. "Because you have been trustworthy in a very small matter, take charge of ten cities."

—Luke 19:17

I love rolling up my sleeves down here on earth and pouring myself into serving God. I'm less of a human being, and more of a human doing. Visiting hospitals, advocating on issues, shopping for dinner, traveling in ministry, relating in marriage, painting at my easel, writing at my computer, working on radio programs, counseling on the phone, helping with Sunday school, and ad infinitum.

I'm also a perfectionist. If a painting is not up to par, it's shoved aside. If an article is not up to snuff, it's dumped in the trash. If a friendship is injured, it's painstakingly repaired. If my marriage is hurting, everything else gets canceled and Ken gets priority. If I feel a speech I give falls flat, I berate myself endlessly, thinking, *Why did I say that? . . . Why didn't I say this?* There have been days when I've thrown up my hands and sighed, "What's the use. I've blown it again!"

But in heaven, there will be no failure in service. No disappointment in doing. We will never struggle with failing to do the task God puts before us. We will never fall short of meeting our responsibilities.

And, boy, will we *do!* No idling away eternity strolling streets of gold. No passing time while plucking harps by the glassy sea. We will have jobs to do. We will serve God through worship and work—exciting work of which we never grow tired.

And if we've been faithful in earthly service, our responsibility in heaven will increase proportionately. No, I take that back. It won't be increased in proportion. God's too generous for that. Our service will increase completely out of proportion. It doesn't take a rocket scientist to read the formula Jesus gives in His heaven parable in Luke 19:17. Those who are faithful in a few minor things will be put in charge over multitudinous things.

Were you faithful in your marriage or a mission? Even if only in a small way? God is already thinking exponentially, as in His "ten cities" equation. The more faithful you are in this life, the more responsibility you will be given in the life to come.

Please note . . . God is not scrutinizing the success of your marriage or judging the results of your mission. You could have spent forty-five years in marriage, forty of which you were hanging in there by a promise and a prayer. You could have invested twenty-five years sharing the gospel in the outback of Mozambique with only a handful of converts to show for it. When it comes to the judgment seat, God won't pull out the return-on-investment charts and do a cost-effectiveness analysis on your earthly service. Every Christian is on the same playing field. Success isn't the key. Faithfulness is.

> **FATHER GOD, I LOVE** serving you. Bring to mind this week something, no matter how small, that I can do for you. Find me faithful in service for you here on earth. ✒

RULING OVER EARTH

Blessed and holy are those who have part in the first resurrection. The second death has no power over them, but they will be priests of God and of Christ and will reign with him for a thousand years.

—Revelation 20:6

We not only get to praise Him forever, but we get to reign with Him forever. Can you believe it? We will be given a sphere of authority and oversight of God's eternal kingdom. We're not talking a few acres on the back of the farm. Our sphere of authority will be heaven and earth. We get to reign over earth with Christ!

It's not clear if it's this earth or what the Bible calls "the new earth." I have to confess I've never had the benefit of going to seminary, and I can't cut as straight a theological line as I'd like, but I'm satisfied just to know that heaven involves earth, old or new. It intrigues me to think that after Christ comes back for us, we may inhabit this very planet again. The paths that I wheel over in my chair now may well be the same ones my glorified feet will walk on when Christ reigns. And the rambling mountain paths behind the Rose Bowl will, in fact, be trod by the heavenly feet of my friend and me.

The possibilities are endless, as well as exhilarating. How about clearing the slums of Rio de Janeiro or getting rid of nuclear waste? Maybe we'll teach the nations how to worship God, as well as a new definition of peace and how to beat their swords into plowshares. Shall we do a patch job on the ozone layer and make the Blue Danube absolute azure rather than mud-brown?

One thing's for sure. There will be no shelters for the homeless. No orphanages or mental hospitals. No abortion clinics. And no nursing homes.

In the midst of it all, the glittering capital city of heaven, the New Jerusalem, will be set like a gleaming pearl. Kings and princes will pour into the Holy City from the far corners of the earth to pay homage. The image blows my mind, but it's laid out as clear as crystal glass in Revelation 21.

How the earth, whether new or old, fits into God's heavenly scheme of things, I can't say for certain. But all I really need to know is "we are looking forward to a new heaven and a new earth, the home of righteousness" (2 Peter 3:13). Heaven will feel like home. I will be a co-heir with Christ. I will help rule in the new heavens and the new earth. I will be busier and happier in service than I ever dreamed possible.

And you will be too.

I'M SO GLAD I'M one of your children, Lord. Not only because of my future reign with you over the earth. Not only because I will reign in heaven too. But because I will be with you for eternity. If that were my only inheritance as a child of God, it would be more than enough. ✒

PART 4

WHERE IS HEAVEN AND
WHAT IS IT LIKE?

> If the way to heaven be narrow, it is
> not long; and if the gate be straight,
> it opens into endless life.
>
> —WILLIAM BEVERIDGE

The universe fascinates me. If there's a program about stars or space exploration on The Discovery Channel, I'm tuned in. Whenever the space shuttle is in orbit, you can find me fixated to the NASA video feed on cable television—I lie in bed and pray over the nations of the world as a little icon of the shuttle moves slowly across a map of the planet.

I watched CNN when the Endeavor astronauts walked in space to make repairs on the Hubble space telescope. Beneath their floating figures lay the earth like a gigantic blue marble. I shook my head in breathless wonder to observe a live picture of our planet slowly turning, with Africa, then the Middle East, then India all gradually rolling by. What was more amazing were the conversations radioed between the shuttle commander and his coworkers as they manipulated the cumbersome telescope.

"Hold this wrench here and put—hey, look over your shoulder. That's Venus behind you." He gave a long, slow whistle. "Man, isn't that beautiful!"

"Watch that screw, it's floating away. Ah-h, would you look at that. There's New Orleans down there."

"Yep, and look, coming up fast, the west coast of Florida."

Like I said, amazing.

With the snap of a finger and a few images from Hubble, astronomers are agreeing that the universe had a beginning. Just like that, Einstein's theory of relativity is proved. And if our complex, highly organized universe had a beginning, it stands to reason that Someone began it. They also agree the universe will have an ending—I wonder if scientists have thought to pick up the book of Revelation for a sneak preview.

I glanced out my window to see the night still ablaze with a parade of brilliant stars. I laid there almost envious of the astronauts who had touched the skirts of space that week. For a while, they had been friends of the stars, tickling the toes of the universe from earth's atmosphere. I yawned a prayer before I drifted back to sleep: "Soon, Jesus, I'll be up there . . . so far beyond . . . and even spacemen won't be able to catch me. . . . Jesus, I'm coming home."

THE TIME OF THE END

But you, Daniel, close up and seal the words of the scroll until the time of the end. Many will go here and there to increase knowledge.

—*Daniel 12:4*

In 1909, my father saw the first Model T Ford chug down Howard Street, and then, months later, the Wright Brothers fly their plane over the Baltimore harbor. He told me it was just too much for his brain. The world was simply going by too fast. My father should have lived to see this day. Millions of gallons of information are being poured into our one-ounce brains as we stare at our planet passing before our eyes.

I wish the prophet Daniel could have lived to see this day too. Then again, maybe he did. Perhaps he saw CNN in some prophetic vision and could only watch in wide-eyed wonder. Maybe his brain could only absorb so much, and he turned away.

Knowledge about our universe is flying at us from right and left. We grasp something new, only to find it obsolete the next time we hear a headliner from some international science conference. Does this proliferation of knowledge mean we've arrived at the time of the end? I wonder if God is unsealing some grand book that has been shut up for centuries in order to reveal, page by page, facts about the heavens that confirm His handiwork.

Scientists used to believe that the universe was full of wandering comets and slow-wheeling galaxies that meandered through space with no rhyme or reason. Now most experts are beginning to acknowledge that a powerful order exists throughout the entire universe, as well as a delicate, yet exact, relationship between forces, fields, and matter. Some dare to call it "beautiful."

It is this delicate and orderly simplicity in the universe that is tugging on the hearts of experts like molecular physicist Dr. John Templeton. He and a handful of others are beginning to turn down the chatter on the scientific debate long enough to hear that haunting echo from the skies.

It is that same song, so ancient and so new, whose notes resound in Psalm 19:1–4: "The heavens declare the glory of God; the skies proclaim the work of his hands. Day after day they pour forth speech; night after night they display knowledge. There is no speech or language where their voice is not heard. Their voice goes out into all the earth, their words to the ends of the world." When we gaze at a starry dome in a nighttime sky, scientists, along with you and me, aren't simply "hearing things." It is a haunting and mesmerizing melody. It is the heavens declaring the glory of God.

LORD, WE'VE LEARNED SO many facts. We've mastered so many formulas. We've harnessed myriad technological advances. Many seem to be going about gaining knowledge for the sake of knowledge alone. Don't let me be caught up in that trap. Grant me instead an insatiable desire for you, your kingdom and my eternal home so that I will be prepared for "the time of the end." 🖋

HOW FAR AWAY IS HEAVEN?

To the LORD your God belong the heavens, even the highest heavens, the earth and everything in it.

—*Deuteronomy 10:14*

As a child I wondered where God lived in outer space and how long it would take to get there. Had I been old enough to read an astronomy textbook, I would have discovered a few statistics which would have blown me out of the water. Our solar system has a diameter of about 700 light-minutes. That's eight billion miles. But the galaxy in which our solar system is contained has a diameter of 100,000 light-years. Not minutes, but *years*. Forget doing the math on that one. Our galaxy is humongous. But here's the kicker: Our little galaxy, which is 100,000 light-years wide, is just *one* of billions of other galaxies out in the cosmos.

I can't comprehend such gargantuan distances nor the breathless enormity of space. Billions of stars and planets, all created by God, most of which the Hubble Space Telescope will never have time to scan. But it's up there on the edge of earth's atmosphere obediently and systematically doing just that—scanning the universe. Hubble has recently captured images close to the very border of our cosmos, and I think it would knock our socks off if it could photograph the actual edge!

What *is* on the other side?

Scientific Journal may be stymied by that question, but not the Bible. Far beyond intergalactic space with its billions of swirling nebulae and novas lies another dimension. Some speculate it's the fifth dimension. You could call it infinity, but wherever it is and however far out, the Bible calls it the highest of heavens. The outermost reaches of space are not as void and lonely as we think, because the highest part of heaven is the abode of God. It would seem this "third heaven," as Scripture calls it, spreads out into infinity and completely engulfs our expanding cosmos with all its celestial bodies. It is the dimension where "the Lord says: 'Heaven is my throne and the earth is my footstool'" (Isaiah 66:1).

The dwelling place of God exists in infinity. It is far, far away. That's why I'm amused when the apostle Paul writes so casually in 2 Corinthians 12:2, "I know a man in Christ who fourteen years ago was caught up to the third heaven."

The third heaven? The highest of heavens? C'mon, Paul, how did you arrive there so fast?

Is heaven a lot closer than we are led to believe?

> **FATHER, I THANK YOU** for the earth that surrounds me. For the trees and sky, for the wind and water, for the creatures and people who inhabit this blue marble I call my earthly home. For the stars and planets and galaxies in our universe, I give you praise. I thank you, too, for the creation I cannot see, taste, feel or touch—the new heaven, the new earth, the endless day. Though these things are far beyond my five senses, I rejoice that they are nearer than I have ever imagined. ✒

69

HOW CLOSE IS HEAVEN?

*Jesus answered him, "I tell you the truth,
today you will be with me in paradise."*

—Luke 23:43

As any good child in Sunday school, I believed that heaven was "up." This is the language the Bible invites us to use, much as it encourages us to use other earthbound words like "crowns" or "seas of glass." And it makes sense. Heaven certainly can't be "down" or we'd dig a hole to China.

Yet even though the dwelling place of God may be a long way up, distances like "up" and "down" lose their meaning when you realize that heaven—even the highest heavens—exist beyond our space-time continuum. Latitude and longitude, as well as directions and distances, are related to time. Time [in heaven] will be swallowed up. Step beyond the edge of outer space and you enter the fifth dimension where gargantuan distances light-years long are a snap of the finger to, well . . . to the dying thief who, when he died, instantly appeared in paradise alongside Jesus.

The Lord gives a clue as to how He does it in Revelation 1:8 when He laughs at time and distance: "'I am the Alpha and Omega,' says the Lord God, 'who is, and who was, and who is to come, the Almighty.'" Notice that Jesus does not follow the convention of our logic about the way time flows; we time-bound creatures want to change the order to read Jesus *was*, is, and is to come. It sounds more chronological. It's consistent with our sense of the past, present, and future. But Jesus is the great "I Am" who always lives in the present. He is the God of the *now*.

So the kingdom of heaven, over which Jesus *is* and was and ever shall be King, is a place, but more so, a dimension where time and distance are not obstacles. The dying thief wasn't transported at superhuman speed to heaven when he died. Rather, he slipped from one dimension to the next, much like Jesus slipped from one room to another, through walls or whatever.

Traveling at a zillion miles per hour might catapult you instantly to the edge of our universe, but to take a step into the third heaven requires more. It requires something different, for our flesh and blood cannot enter heaven. When the dying thief was born of the Spirit, he was given the spiritual "genes," so to speak, of God Himself—Christ who *is*, was, and ever shall be.

You cannot be *transported* to heaven. You couldn't even go there in a time machine, if there were such a thing. You must be born again or you cannot, as Jesus warned, "see the kingdom of God." When we are Spirit-born we, like the thief, are fit for eternity.

Heaven is close. Perhaps closer than we imagine.

LORD, IT'S HARD TO understand how heaven can be so close yet farther away than the edges of this universe. Like the rays of the sun that pierce the dark clouds in the sky so let the reality of heaven's nearness, and yours, break through the darkened understanding of my mind. ✒

WHERE IS HEAVEN?

So we fix our eyes not on what is seen, but on what is unseen. For what is seen is temporary, but what is unseen is eternal.

—*2 Corinthians 4:18*

Heaven is close. It's a little like saying to an unborn infant in his mother's womb, "Do you realize that you are about to be born into a great big world full of mountains, rivers, and a sun and a moon? In fact, you exist in that wonderful world right now."

Dear baby! There he is, safe in his little world, ignorant of the fact that a more glorious world is enclosing and encasing his. A world for which he is being fashioned. Only when he is birthed into it will he comprehend that all along his warm dark world was within it. This other place of wonderful beauty was present all the time. Only inches away.

Actually, at this moment, less than a hairsbreadth separates this material world from the spiritual world that is embracing earth. And like an unborn baby, we are being fashioned for the greater world into which we are about to be born (by dying, of all things!). We have a hard time believing that heaven encompasses this world, and so the Bible has to keep prodding us to fix our eyes "not on what is seen, but what is unseen." It's a matter of "seeing." Using our eyes of faith.

Faith assures us that heaven is *transcendent*. It is beyond the limits of our experience; it exists apart from our material universe. Heaven is also *immanent* in that it envelopes all the celestial bodies, swirling galaxies, and the starry hosts. If we believe that God is omnipresent, then we can at least believe that what the Bible in Ephesians 2:6 calls the heavenly realms are omnipresent, as well. For where God is, the kingdom of heaven is.

Heaven is closer than we imagine even though we can't see it. I can almost see God laughing at people's propensity to fix their eyes only on that which is seen, when in Jeremiah 23:23–24 He reminds us, "'Am I only a God nearby,' declares the Lord, 'and not a God far away?'"

One day we will take the same trip as the dying thief. We will arrive in Paradise. In the meantime we can say we operate in the realm of our omnipresent and sovereign God. In some respects, we exist in the kingdom of heaven now. There's a significant part of us, the "new creature in Christ," which lives in the present tense. Very much like our great "I Am."

This fact makes the far and distant, near and oh so close. When we seize this reality, we understand that the air we breathe is celestial. The ground we tread is sacred. The light we enjoy is divine. Could the rustling in the trees even be the whisper of angel wings? That's touching on romanticism, but as the Bible itself says, "[We] have come to thousands upon thousands of angels in joyful assembly" (Hebrews 12:22).

Literally.

> Open my eyes, that I may see
> Glimpses of truth Thou hast for me; . . .
> Open my eyes, illumine me, Spirit divine!
>
> —Clara H. Scott

ANGELS ALL AROUND

*And Elisha prayed, "O LORD, open his
eyes so he may see." Then the LORD
opened the servant's eyes, and he looked
and saw the hills full of horses and char-
iots of fire all around Elisha.*

—*2 Kings 6:17*

Recently I took part in a nationwide prayer rally across Canada,
which linked together Christian audiences by live satellite television. I wheeled into the cavernous sports arena. The place was echo-
ing with the sounds of workmen hammering and ushers rehearsing.
We all knew that the next morning thousands of intercessors would
fill the arena to shake the heavenly realms with their prayers.

When it came time for my sound check, I wheeled to the
microphone on the wooden platform. "Testing, testing," I said
as my voice boomed across the arena.

My eyes scanned the empty seats. While the sound man continued his work, I began to pray into the microphone, "Lord, we know
that this arena has been the scene of everything from ice hockey
fights to drug deals during rock concerts. There are a lot of fallen
angels, a lot of demons hanging around here, I can sense it."

I continued to pray, this time a little louder so my amplified voice would reach the rafters. And as I did, some of the workmen stopped their drilling, and most of the ushers took seats and bowed their heads. "Jesus, You told us in Your Word that whatever we bind on earth would be bound in heaven, and whatever we loose on earth would be released in heaven. So in Your name, we ask You to clear this place of evil spirits. Dispatch big, powerful angels with swords drawn and shields held high to stand guard over this place. Make this sports arena a house of prayer."

Skeptics wave you off and say that such a prayer is a nice token, but merely conciliatory. Christians know better. The "kingdom of the air" is heavily populated with spiritual beings; and although we only have a hint in Ephesians 2:2 or 6:12, we know that they are real, powerful, and present.

But not as powerful as angels. Perhaps the reality of heaven would spring to life for us if we could peel away this layer, which is only as thick as a thin veil, and take a peek.

That once actually happened to the servant of the prophet Elisha. He was struck with terror at the sight of the massive Syrian force that had come by night. Elisha's reply was calm: "Do not fear, for those who are with us are more than those who are with them." And then Elisha prayed that his servant's eyes might be opened to see the heavenly realities all around him.

What was true for Elisha is true for any believer. I wish our eyes could be opened to see the heavenly realms all around us. Our eyes would pop at all the hosts of angels and ministering spirits—a few of which are most likely within a hairsbreadth next to you now.

> **LORD, YOU'VE SAID YOUR** angels are all around me. Help me to take comfort, as Elisha's servant did, in knowing that I'm never alone and never outnumbered. 🖋

OUR RELATIONSHIP TO ANGELS

*Are not all angels ministering spirits sent
to serve those who will inherit salvation?*

—Hebrews 1:14

The more heavenly minded I become, the more convinced I am of the presence of angels in my life. Their job description has included bringing messages. They aid in answering prayer, as they did with Daniel. Angels bring with them something of the presence of God, as well as help the Lord shape history. They really shine when it comes to protecting or delivering us. Suffice to say, they're busy.

One of the best parts of heaven may be getting to know and fellowshiping with angels. They love God and they enjoy us. In a parable about sinners gaining entrance into the kingdom of heaven, Jesus said, "I tell you, there is rejoicing in the presence of the angels of God over one sinner who repents" (Luke 15:10). If angels rejoiced so happily over our conversion, how much more will they rejoice over us when we arrive at the foot of God's throne. They will see our redemption completed, from beginning to end.

Angels will also serve us in heaven. We will reign with Jesus; and if He has been given authority over all the heavenly hosts, then we will reign over angels too. It's thrilling to imagine. We'll be able to rally angelic legions, as well as lead the way in doing God's work in heaven and on earth.

We will also worship with the angels. They've had a lot of practice at worshiping, as well as access to heaven's throne. They've seen it all. Yet when we arrive in heaven, it will be *their* privilege to worship with us. Just think what our worship will sound like. In Revelation 5:11–13, angels crowd before the throne, "numbering thousands upon thousands, and ten thousand times ten thousand. . . . In a loud voice they sang: 'Worthy is the Lamb, who was slain, to receive power and wealth and wisdom and strength and honor and glory and praise!'"

Every time I read that verse, I recall a marvelous experience at the Moody Pastor's Conference. I was told that the singing would be out of this world. And it was. When I wheeled onto the platform I scanned the auditorium of 1,800 men.

The song leader had the men stand up, spread out into the aisles, and fill the stage. When they held hymnbooks high and broke into a rousing chorus, a jet blast of sound hit me head-on.

Never had I been so utterly surrounded by sound. It was pure and powerful, clear and deep. A thunderous waterfall of perfect bass and baritone, so passionate it made my heart break.

It was a moment of ecstasy, so serendipitous and God-anointed, that I had to step outside myself and be carried heavenward. If this earthly choir moved me, how much more when our voices blend with the angels!

I THANK YOU, LORD, for the angels you send to protect and comfort me. Your servant here on earth is looking forward to the soon coming day of fellowshiping around your throne with your heavenly servants. What a joyous celebration that will be! ✒

WE WILL JUDGE ANGELS

Do you not know that we will judge angels? How much more the things of this life!

—*1 Corinthians 6:3*

This short but powerful Scripture is another one of those exponential statements that smack of an almost unbelievable increase in our capacity to serve, as well as our responsibility in ruling. When it comes to fallen angels—demons—we will judge them. Once again, God will blow out all formulas on proportions and put us in charge of judging fallen angels. I cringe at the idea, because on earth I'm having a tough enough time deciding who's right in a friendly spat or who ought to get the last piece of pie or whether or not justice was served in a local court case.

Me? Judging angels? Again, I breathe a sigh of relief to know that I will have all of God's wisdom at my disposal; otherwise, the job would send me cowering. It's just another way we will rule with Christ in heaven.

Frankly, the idea intrigues me. There are a couple of evil spirits I can't wait to nail. On earth, I have been so harassed by troublesome demons of temptation or evil forces who keep trying to trip me up.

I'm not saying "the devil made me do it" on earth; I take full responsibility for my choices and actions. But demons sure haven't helped.

Then there are the more heinous powers and principalities of darkness who have incited wicked men to wreak havoc. These are the gruesome chief demons under Satan who for centuries have pushed evil men further into rebellion, murder, torture, and grisly massacres. And especially those forces of evil who instigated the treason and injustice behind the crucifixion of God's own Son.

When I see news magazine photos of mutilated children in Rwanda, old women beaten in Bosnia, or twisted bodies in a bombed-out building in Oklahoma City, I naturally get mad at people who do such things. But when you consider who's behind it all, I don't vent anger at God, I get furious with the devil and his cohorts. The psalmist was speaking of evil men in Psalm 139:22, but I'll throw in fallen angels and say, "I have nothing but hatred for them; I count them my enemies."

These demons have had a heyday on earth. I see their trademark on everything from pornography spewed from magazines to the humanism spouted from elementary school textbooks. Most of all, it hurts when I see men and women gripped in the claws of spiritism and the occult; Satan has blinded their eyes.

I'm one hundred percent behind virtually every sermon Jonathan Edwards preached about hellfire and brimstone, the place God created for the devil and his followers. I can hardly wait for that glorious—yes, glorious—day when Satan and his legions will be punished and eternally tormented for their procuring the fall of mankind. One day we shall have the pleasure of demonstrating "perfect hatred," as Scripture puts it, against the rulers, powers, and principalities of darkness.

This humbles me before God.

And yes, I hate the devil.

WILL THERE BE ENVY IN HEAVEN?

*For where you have envy and selfish
ambition, there you find disorder and
every evil practice. But the wisdom that
comes from heaven is first of all pure;
then peace-loving, considerate, submis-
sive, full of mercy and good fruit, impar-
tial and sincere.*

—James 3:16-17

I'm speechless. I am awed and inspired by the fact that what I do on earth will have a direct bearing on how I will serve God in heaven. Sometimes I feel like I'm in the minor leagues, working hard to be ensured a berth somewhere in the major leagues in heaven. I'm not talking about earning salvation, but about earning a reward. It affects everything from how much heart will go into my eternal worship of God to the kind of job I'll be assigned on the new earth. It even affects the way I'll govern angels to my capacity for eternal joy and possibly the extent of my appreciation for all that Jesus has done for me and others here on earth.

And as far as envy is concerned, don't worry. It won't happen in heaven. Remember, we will be totally transformed. Envy will be an impossibility. No competing and no comparison in heaven. Still, it makes perfect sense that God will exalt those whom He chooses to honor. It's His prerogative. Whomever He chooses to lift up is fine with me. I'll be more than happy for the godly men and women whom Christ will elevate as the most celebrated pillars in His temple.

When it comes to heaven, I'm convinced the highest accolades will go—and should go—to godly people who have labored loyally yet received no recognition. I can't wait for the Lord to greatly honor the missionary in the back jungles of Brazil who spent fifteen years translating Scripture and then quietly moved on to the next tribe to do the same. I want to see the Lord richly reward small-town pastors who faithfully preached every Sunday morning despite meager numbers in the pews. Better yet, pastors in China who are still suffering persecution and haven't seen the light of day from their jail cells in years.

I hope the Lord takes highest delight in elderly grandmothers in nursing homes who didn't dwell on their plight, but rather prayed, without fanfare, for others. Godly teenagers who held fast to their virginity, saying "no" time and again to peer pressure, intimidation, and their hormones. And moms and dads of handicapped children who, in the name of Jesus, served the family faithfully despite the day-to-day routine, isolation, and financial setbacks.

These are the real heroes and heroines over whom we will be exceedingly glad to hear the Lord say, "Well done, good and faithful servant!" When they receive their reward, I'll stand happily on the sidelines, cheering, whistling, and applauding wildly. I may have stood up to the vicissitudes of human hardship, like pain and paralysis, but their strength of spirit more than matched, even way surpassed, mine. And do you know what will thrill me most? The obedience of these unsung heroes will raise the wattage on God's glory. He will shine brighter because of them.

My Capacity for Eternal Joy

*And the ransomed of the LORD will
return. They will enter Zion with singing;
everlasting joy will crown their heads.
Gladness and joy will overtake them, and
sorrow and sighing will flee away.*

—Isaiah 35:10

In heaven, your capacity for joy will be filled to overflowing.
Your reward will be your capacity—your capacity for joy, service, and worship. Jonathan Edwards described these capacities
this way: "The saints are like so many vessels of different sizes
cast into a sea of happiness where every vessel is full: this is eternal life, for a man ever to have his capacity filled."

When I think of my vessel, I picture a gallon bucket into
which the Lord will pour His joy until it gushes over the brim,
bubbling up and effervescing. I'll laugh with delight for others
who will have a joy-capacity the size of a big bath tub, or a tanker
truck, or a silo. Like me, they will be filled to overflowing, and
we all shall be as happy as cats with nine tails!

Whether a small vial or a large vase, we shall all be spilling
and splashing over with the joy of the Lord; and even those

whose capacity is only the size of a thimble won't know jealousy. We shall be fat, sassy, and satiated with joy. Constant brimming over. Happiness unspeakable in worship and service. Each of us will have complete contentment for the station our Master has allocated us in eternal life.

So, I'm fixing my eyes on Jesus and focusing on things unseen. I'm stretching my heart's capacity for God here on earth to insure my bucket for joy in heaven will be deep and wide. I'm searching high and low in my heart to choose the right building materials, whether it be gold, silver, precious stones, or platinum-plated service.

I have a clear conscience in light of 1 Corinthians 9:24, which encourages missionaries, prisoners, teenagers, moms and dads, all of us in the contest to "run in such a way as to get the prize."

Is it selfish to run hard in order to gain the prize? Is working toward rewards mercenary? Certainly not. Heavenly crowns are not just rewards for a job well done on earth; if your focus is on Jesus, they are the glorious fulfillment of the job itself. Just like marriage is the reward and the happy consummation of love, and a medal of honor is the reward given at the end of a victorious battle, so it will be with heaven's crowns. A reward is the cherry and whipped-cream topping of the pleasure of serving God down here on earth. It is the joy of sticking to the call He gave at the beginning.

Heaven is one big reward. Gift after gift after gift.

> Be joyful in the Lord, my heart!
> Both soul and body bear your part:
> To God all praise and glory!
>
> — Johann J. Schütz

PART 5

WHY DON'T WE FIT ON EARTH?

> The way to Heaven is ascending; we
> must be content to travel up hill,
> though it be hard and tiresome, and
> contrary to the natural bias of our
> flesh.
>
> — JONATHAN EDWARDS

It was mayhem. My friend was steering me in my wheelchair through thick crowds and piles of suitcases in the baggage claim area of the Los Angeles airport. Angry passengers bemoaned lost luggage. A line of people jostled through a turnstile. Outside, taxis honked. Policemen hollered. It was a crazy ending to an even crazier day of bad weather and a late arrival. We found our luggage carousel, and my friend parked my chair to go retrieve our things.

While I waited in the midst of pandemonium, I did what I always do. I waited and sat still. Very still. It's a fact of life. Because I'm paralyzed from the shoulders down, a large part of me never moves. I have instant stillness. I don't run, I sit. I don't race, I wait. Even when rushing, I stay put in my wheelchair. I could be scurrying through a jam-packed schedule, doing this and that, but a big part of me—due to my paralysis—is always quiet.

That's why, if you had seen me in that busy airport, you would have noticed a satisfied smile. Perhaps in an earlier time I would have felt trapped, useless, and resentful that I could not grab my own suitcase, elbow the guy who butted in line, or hail my own taxi. But faith, honed and sharpened from years in my wheelchair, has changed that. And so, I sat there thanking God for built-in quiet and stillness before Him.

I also thought about heaven. With eyes of faith I looked beyond the sight of bumper-to-bumper traffic, the smell of sweat, cigarettes, exhaust fumes, and the sounds of my harried co-travelers, and began humming quietly . . .

For me, it was a moment of faith. Faith merely the size of a grain of mustard seed. Remember, that's all it takes to be sure of things hoped for—future divine fulfillments—and certain of things you do not see, that is, unseen divine realities.

Of what was I so sure and certain? "This world is not my home, I'm just a passing through, . . . And I can't feel at home in this world anymore."

NOT MY HOME

Instead, they were longing for a better country—a heavenly one. Therefore God is not ashamed to be called their God, for he has prepared a city for them.

—Hebrews 11:16

I definitely feel "this world is not my home" as I sit on the Ventura-Freeway-turned-parking-lot. Sometimes I get that "can't feel at home" sensation ambling down the aisles of K-Mart, watching women grab for the blue-light specials. Sometimes it happens sitting with Ken watching Monday Night Football's fourth instant replay of a team's third-down conversion.

Don't think I'm strange. Christians have felt the same for centuries. Malcolm Muggeridge, a British journalist who spent most of his years battling Christianity, finally succumbed to Christ in his seventies. The intellectual world had always been home to him, but now, in the hallowed halls of university life, he found himself saying, "I had a sense, sometimes enormously vivid, that I was a stranger in a strange land; a visitor, not a native."

His words could have been mine as I wheeled through the Thousand Oaks Mall yesterday. I was a stranger in a strange land between the video game parlor on the second floor and the first floor movie complex running the latest Arnold Schwartzenegger film. Actually, I felt like a blessed stranger. A displaced, but satisfied person. Everyone seemed absorbed by the fashion show going on in the center courtyard, but I found myself thinking, *Does anyone else here realize that there's more to life than the new fall designs?*

That's what blessed strangers and satisfied displaced persons feel. They see that heaven is *home*. It's where we belong.

I did not feel at home in that mall. I did not belong. I saw its world as trite and commonplace. My heart went out to the kids hanging around the video parlor and the ladies watching the fashion show. The troubling part was the "world" in which they were engrossed. My heart especially went out to a teenage girl in jeans and plaid shirt who was staring enviously at the gaunt figure of a female mannequin who stared back at her through lifeless eyes. That said it all.

I couldn't help but see something past this world. How so? Because faith is double-sided. It not only verifies heaven as real, giving hard and fast reality to that which we do not see, but it also makes us look differently at visible things on earth. Through faith's eyes, heaven becomes a rock-solid home, and the concrete world in which we live becomes drained of substance and importance. When we look at life through eyes of faith, things around us no longer possess the glow of excitement.

Because faith makes invisible things real, and visible things unreal, earthly dissatisfaction becomes the road to heavenly satisfaction. One place, heaven, supplants the other, earth, as home.

LORD, THE BEST THINGS of this world don't even minutely stack up to the wonderful things you have planned for me in heaven. Better than beautiful sunrises and glowing sunsets. Better than crashing surf and waterfalls. Thank you for sparing no expense when it comes to preparing a place for me. ✒

ALIENS, STRANGERS AND MISFITS

*All these people were still living by faith
when they died. They did not receive the
things promised; they only saw them and
welcomed them from a distance. And
they admitted that they were aliens and
strangers on earth.*

—*Hebrews 11:13*

The more homelike heaven becomes, the more you feel like an
alien and stranger on earth. "Our citizenship is in heaven"
(Philippians 3:19–20). I'm not talking spiritual snobbery here.
It's simply a matter of focus: "For where your treasure is, there
your heart will be also" (Matthew 6:21).

This feeling of being an alien or stranger on earth has more
to do with the song I told you about. The haunting echo.

I'm a little like a refugee longing for my better country. My heart
is in quasi-exile. In fact, 1 Kings 11:14–22 is "me" all over. It seems
that Hadad, an adversary of Solomon, had fled for safety to Egypt
with some of his father's family. There he found great favor with
Pharaoh, married into the king's family, and reared his son in the
royal palace. But when he heard that David was dead, "Hadad said
to Pharaoh, 'Let me go, that I may return to my own country.'"

"'What have you lacked here that you want to go back to your own country?' Pharaoh asked."

"'Nothing,' Hadad replied, 'but do let me go!'"

That's the part I identify with. Earth may be rich with past memories and present moments as it was with Hadad, but I'm hot on his heels: "Let me go, that I may return to my own country." It is always the exiles who remember home. The Israelites, captive in a foreign land, remembered their true country when they mourned in Psalm 137:1: "By the rivers of Babylon we sat and wept when we remembered Zion." Like Hadad, like the Israelites, I carry in my exiled heart a hunger for my heavenly country, my soul's true home.

A person who feels at home "fits" with his environment, like a fish in water, a bird in the sky, or a worm in the dirt. But we don't "fit" here. It's not our environment. There is no harmony, no "rightness," with our surroundings. Remember my experiences in the Los Angeles airport and the Thousand Oaks Mall? It wasn't as though the hustle and bustle of that world offended me; it's just that it didn't jibe, it didn't resonate with the peace and stillness in my heart, a peace that echoed, "You don't belong here."

> O Lord, I live here as a fish in a vessel of water,
> only enough to keep me alive,
> but in heaven I shall swim in the ocean.
> Here I have a little air in me to keep me breathing,
> but there I shall have sweet and fresh gales;
> Here I have a beam of sun to lighten my darkness,
> a warm ray to keep me from freezing;
> yonder I shall live in light and warmth forever.

> —A Puritan prayer

WHY DON'T WE FIT?

*There is a time for everything, and a sea-
son for every activity under heaven: a
time to be born and a time to die, a time
to plant and a time to uproot.*

—Ecclesiastes 3:1-2

As Christians, you and I are not made for this world.

Well, in one sense we are. Our hands, feet, eyes, and ears equip
us for physical experiences on this planet made of water and dirt.
Our ears process noise, our eyes register sights, our noses detect
odors, and our stomachs digest food. But we are also spirit. This
makes for incredible tension. Someone once said, "Through faith
we understand that we are not physical beings having a spiritual
experience, but spiritual beings having a physical experience."

You and I are not made for this world because the earth is
temporal. There is something in us that is definitely *not* temporal. That's why we squirm and groan against the confines of time.
The clock, for us, is an adversary. Every heavenly moment—
whether it be gazing into the soft eyes and gentle smile of the
one we love or relishing the ecstasy of some glorious pleasure—
every moment like this we embrace so we might keep time at

bay. But we can't. We would like to call these moments timeless, but they're not. Time snatches them from our grasp.

This is where the tension *really* kicks in. Time is our natural environment, yet time is *not* our natural environment.

It's not just Christians who kick against the traces of time. People who don't believe in God consider time an adversary. For them, the ticking of the second hand sounds like the stalking of an enemy. Each minute moves them toward death. And everyone, whether rich or poor, tries to grab the hour hand to shove it backward. "Slow down and live" is a slogan on everything from highway signs to health books. But we can't slow down time. Wrinkle cream won't do it. Pumping your brain and brawn with vitamins E and A won't do it. And freezing your body in an iced hydrogen chamber won't stop time either.

All of humanity senses this, for, "He has also set eternity in the hearts of men; yet they cannot fathom what God has done from beginning to end" (Ecclesiastes 3:11). Yes, people in general just can't fathom God, let alone this thing about a timeless eternity. They don't know what to do with it except to buy Shirley MacLaine's latest New Age best-seller or apply more Oil of Olay. Their only real recourse against the onslaught of time is their memories.

You and I are not made for this world.

LORD, TIME IS MY enemy on days like today when there is so much to accomplish. But if it were not for time there would be no blessing in the changing of seasons, things to look forward to and fond memories of bygone days. Thank you that you have made me a finite creature. Help me to find the blessings hidden within the constraints of my allotted time here on earth. ✒

LONGING FOR ANOTHER TIME

He has also set eternity in the hearts of men; yet they cannot fathom what God has done from beginning to end.

—Ecclesiastes 3:11b

When I was first paralyzed in 1967—and still new to this eternity thing as a young Christian—heaven was in no way my home. I was less interested in looking forward to a glorified body and more interested in turning back the clock to days when my body worked. Time was also an enemy in that it kept putting more distance between the past on my feet and the present in my wheelchair.

I couldn't do much but listen to the radio or records. I laid on the Stryker frame in the intensive care unit and tuned into Diana Ross moaning about a lost love or Glen Campbell crooning about an old flame wandering on the back roads of his memory. The Beatles were also popular then. I would fight back the tears when they'd sing of a yesterday when troubles seemed so far away.

Then there was Joni Mitchell. I found refuge in her restless songs about the past. Her music evoked a more powerful and fundamental nostalgia than pining for a lost love or a trouble-free yesterday. Joni Mitchell and thousands like her are looking for something incalculably precious they've lost, something they've got to get back to. They may mistake it for the nostalgia of the sixties or the fifties; they may mistake it for a childhood memory, a lost love, or a yesterday when one's troubles seemed so far away, but it's much more than that. It's a nostalgia not for the innocence of youth, but for the innocence of humanity. "We've got to get ourselves back to the Garden," a lost world groans, because it's Eden where we lost not just our youth, but our identity.

We may not realize it, but the whole of humanity is exiled from the bliss of the intimate presence of God, "walking in the Garden in the cool of the evening." Most people don't understand that to walk with God is to feel at home.

Even if people could reach back into the Garden, if Joni Mitchell could go back to the moment of the creation of the world, it wouldn't be enough. She'd stand there in the middle of a perfect environment and feel perfectly ill at ease, not realizing satisfaction could only be found by taking one more step off the edge of time itself and into the mind of God. Even those who do not hope for heaven still wrestle with this vexing enigma of "eternity" set in their heart.

Most people have it backward.

Unlike those who don't believe in God, our road is not back to the Garden of Eden, but forward. Our nostalgia for Eden is not just for another time, but another *kind* of time. One should never look over one's shoulder on the road of hope.

> Hallelujah! I have found Him
>> Whom my soul so long has craved!
> Jesus satisfies my longings—
>> Through His blood I now am saved.
>
> —Clara T. Williams

OUR TRUE IDENTITY

He who has an ear, let him hear what the Spirit says to the churches. To him who overcomes, I will give some of the hidden manna. I will also give him a white stone with a new name written on it, known only to him who receives it.

—*Revelation 2:17*

Only in heaven—the birthplace of our identity—will we find out who we truly are. Our true identity will unfold in the new name God will give us. You will not only find what was irretrievably lost, but when you receive it—your new name, your true identity—you will be a thousand times more yourself than the sum total of all those nuances, gestures, and inside subtleties that defined the earthbound "you." On earth you may think you fully blossomed, but heaven will reveal that you barely budded.

What's more, you will be like none other in heaven. The fact that no one else has your name shows how utterly unique you are to God. You touch His heart in a way no one else can. It is a royal seal of His individual love on you.

You have a specific place niched in heaven—in God's heart—which fits you and you alone. In heaven you will reflect Him like a facet of a diamond, and people will say to you, "I *love* seeing that part of God in you."

Everyone else will receive their true identity too. They also will reflect God in unique and complete ways. C. H. Spurgeon suggested this is why redeemed people will number more than the grains of sand on the beach or the stars in the sky. An endless number of saints will be required to fully reflect the infinite facets of God's love. Could it be that without you, some wonderful nuance of God's love, dare I say, might not get reflected were you not in heaven?

United in perfect praise and love, we will finally and fully discover who we are, where we belong, and what God destined us to do—and we will have all of eternity to be and do that very thing.

In heaven, you will discover rich, wonderful things about the true identity of your husband, wife, daughter, son, brother, sister, or special friends, things that were only hinted at on earth. What's more, you will *know* them like you never knew them on earth. You will exclaim to your loved one, "Wow, so *this* is what I loved in you for so long!" for you will see him or her as God intended all along.

Only believers who understand that the coordinates converge in eternity can sing, "This world is not my home." We are pilgrims becoming, in the here and now, who we shall be in the hereafter.

So onward we pilgrims tread through this world of time and death, forever seeking the Son. We don't go backward but, "Forgetting what is behind and straining toward what is ahead, [we] press on toward the goal to win the prize for which God has called [us] heavenward in Christ Jesus" (Philippians 3:13–14).

Hallelujah!

Our Place in Time

Flesh gives birth to flesh, but the Spirit gives birth to spirit.

—*John 3:6*

Jesus is the only One who was ever comfortable with His identity, as well as comfortable in or out of time. Jesus, having both a divine and human nature, presented a kind of formula for our nature and destiny. The way our resurrected Lord was able to move through time and space is a prescription for our future heavenly experience. Jesus perfectly embodies physical things caught in time yet spiritual things that exist outside of time.

One second Jesus could be conversing with friends on the road to Emmaus, the next He could bypass the hours required to travel to Jerusalem and appear there in no time flat. Stone walls and unopened doors in the Upper Room presented no barriers. Time, space, and therefore distance were, for Him, a cinch. His ability to move in and out of various dimensions clues us into where time fits in heaven. I don't think heaven will destroy time, so much as swallow it up.

Time will be folded into eternity and lose its distinction much like egg whites when they are folded into cream. Or more to the point, like folding one egg white into an ocean of cream. That's how all-encompassing eternity is.

How long would staring at a dot on a piece of paper hold your interest? If you can say five seconds, I'm impressed. But what if you placed a pen on that dot and drew a line to create a two-dimensional stick figure? That's a bit more interesting, but certainly not as provocative as observing a three-dimensional sculpture of that figure, right? If it's a good sculpture, it might hold your attention for a long time. A sculpture is a far cry from being as fascinating as a real live human being who moves through time and space in the fourth dimension. It's a fact that each dimension is more interesting than the previous.

Now carry this little formula through to the fifth dimension, heaven. All the wondrous things about the previous dimensions will be in heaven, plus a whole lot more. This means heaven will be *extremely* interesting. It will be irresistible, enravishing, intriguing, and at least ten more columns of adjectives. The exotic peacock, the perfect hexagons in beehives, the aquamarine of a tropical lagoon, the orangutan who makes us giggle, and the inspiring snowcapped peaks of the Alps are all part of the fourth dimension. And—ta-dah—the fifth one is about to be revealed! Heaven will be far beyond all the beauty of earth combined.

Who knows what wonders the fifth dimension, and probably many other dimensions, will contain. In eternity everything is just a beginning. No borders. No limits. Can you now see why Paul says, "No eye has seen, no ear has heard, no mind has conceived what God has prepared for those who love him" (1 Corinthians 3:9)?

> **LORD, ENLARGE MY SPIRIT.** Nurture the living, eternal, God-created spirit you have placed in me. Grow me up in you that I might be to the praise of your glory. ✐

UNSEEN REALITIES

We live by faith, not by sight.

—2 Corinthians 5:7

This dusty little planet keeps spinning through time and deep dark space, not realizing that all the while it is swimming in the ocean of eternity and surrounded by a host of unseen divine realities and divine fulfillments. But we realize it because as pilgrims "we live by faith, not by sight" (2 Corinthians 5:7). By faith we live on a different plane, in another dimension, at a higher level than the earthly one. By faith the rock-solid world becomes drained of substance and importance, and we see a heavenly meaning behind *everything*.

People who lack faith look at the front range of the Rocky Mountains and assume, in a mechanistic way, that a tectonic plate pushed this way and that, causing a quake and a shifting in the earth's crust then—voilà—there appeared Pikes Peak. But pilgrims heading for heaven realize that "by him all things were created: things in heaven and on earth, visible and invisible, whether thrones or powers or rulers or authorities; all things were created by him and for him" (Colossians 1:16). He has created invisible things that are just as real—no, *more* real—than the Rocky Mountains. No wonder we praise our Creator!

People who lack faith look at a beautiful cherry tree, shrug their shoulders, and suppose a seed fell, rain poured, roots sprouted, a sapling grew, and soon it shall be someone's firewood. God, they think, just wound nature up like a clock to let it tick-tock on its way. People with heaven-inspired faith look at the same tree and marvel that literally "in him all things hold together" (Colossians 1:17). That means *all* things. Right now. This instant. Even buds, bark, and branches.

Those with an earthly perspective assume that the waves of the sea are made up of plain old H2O, but those with a heavenly point of view believe that every proton on the Periodic Table of the Elements is held together by God, for He is "sustaining all things by his powerful word" (Hebrews 1:3). Let that fact sink in. If God were to withdraw His command, the mountains, oceans, and trees wouldn't collapse into chaos, they would go poof and disappear! God's creation isn't static and inert, it's dynamic and actually in the process of being sustained this instant by His powerful word.

And when it comes to the marvel of the human body, those who have no faith claim we've risen out of slime to the status of homo erectus, and assume that humans draw breath under their own power. But pilgrims with a heart for heaven know differently, "for in him we live and move and have our being" (Acts 17:28). In heaven we will be more human than what our species only hinted of here. We will be more the man or the woman than what our gender only whispered of.

> Earth's crammed with heaven,
> And every common bush afire with God;
> But only he who sees takes off his shoes,
> The rest sit 'round it and pluck blackberries.
>
> —Elizabeth Barrett Browning

TOO HEAVENLY MINDED

Since, then, you have been raised with Christ, set your hearts on things above, where Christ is seated at the right hand of God.

—Colossians 3:1

When a Christian realizes his citizenship is in heaven, he begins acting as a responsible citizen of earth. He invests wisely in relationships because he knows they're eternal. He gives generously of time, money, and talent because he's laying up treasures for eternity. All this serves the pilgrim well not only in heaven, but on earth; for it serves everyone around him.

A few weeks ago I went to the Hair and Nail Shoppe to get a haircut. What does a pilgrim do in an average ordinary place like this? Sojourners look for the unseen divine realities around them. As the stylist whipped the plastic cape over me, I glanced around at the other women. I tried to put myself in the shoes of these women, looking for their "realities"—divorce, dieting, raising children. A few professional types in their power suits in for a quick repair on a fingernail were dealing with different "realities"—promotions, payoffs, and executive stress.

I knew God had His own divine realities in mind for each woman. So, sitting with my hair all wet, I interceded off and on for each person, setting in motion God's powerful workings in their lives. This is the way ordinary pilgrims make themselves of some earthly good.

My husband, Ken, lives like this. He's been fostering a relationship with two young gas-station attendants from Iran. Most people are in and out for a quick fill-up, but Ken keeps his eyes open for the unseen divine realities at work in the lives of these two men. He's one heaven-minded person looking for ways to do earth some good.

Besides this, pilgrims do battle. Ken and I helped chaperone the prom of the public high school where he teaches. The early hours of the prom were a great time to connect with students, admire their tuxedos, and wish them well at college. After dinner, though, the lights went out, the music went up, and the ballroom reverted into a wild disco. Through the dark and deafening noise I spotted a senior girl in a skimpy white-sequined dress sitting on her boyfriend's knee. I decided to pray for her. Silently mouthing my prayer, it struck me that although the ballroom was shaking, my prayer was more powerful than the 600-amp Bose speakers angled over the dance floor. A simple intercession was shaking and sending repercussions across heaven.

This is how heaven's citizens live while temporarily residing on earth. Heaven tells us every person, place, and thing has a purpose. This is why "we fix our eyes not on what is seen, but what is unseen. For what is seen is temporary, but what is unseen is eternal" (2 Corinthians 5:18).

LORD, HELP ME AS I aim for heaven. Cultivate within me a useful affection for heaven that will benefit me and others here on earth. Keep me heavenly minded *and* earthly good.

HOMESICK FOR HEAVEN

Meanwhile we groan, longing to be clothed with our heavenly dwelling.

—2 Corinthians 5:2

The faith of which I've been speaking imparts heavenly purpose to everything—absolutely everything—around us. This happens to me every Tuesday, Wednesday, and Thursday morning when my artist friend, Patti, helps get me out of bed. Before I get in the van and she sends me off to work, we pause at the opened garage door and take a few moments to observe the day.

The other day Patti commented on a hibiscus bloom, reminding us, "God dreamed up that color! Perhaps just for the sheer fun of it." Pilgrims see His delight in giving us pleasure. Heavenly sojourners see God in everything; they see that every bush they pass on earth's wilderness is a burning bush, afire with God. And with such faith it is truly possible to please Him (Hebrews 11:6).

One of the very last things Jesus says in the final chapter of Revelation is, "Behold, I am coming soon!" Revelation 22, when Jesus says three times to the waiting church, "I am coming soon!" (To which the church replies three times, "Come!") It's interesting He doesn't say, "I will come . . . like, sometime around, oh, a couple of thousand years from now." Jesus puts it in the present tense as though He were but a hairsbreadth away, all ready to part the veil of time and distance and step back into our world. It's as though He were on His way back now.

Don't think such heavenly mindedness makes us pilgrims no earthly good. We pilgrims walk the tightrope between earth and heaven, feeling trapped in time, yet with eternity beating in our hearts. Our pilgrimage to heaven is not a journey toward the end of time, but to another kind of time. Our unsatisfied sense of exile is not to be solved or fixed while here on earth. Our pain and longings make sure we will never be content, but that's good: it is to our benefit that we do not grow comfortable in a world destined for decay.

And so we squirm and writhe, knowing we don't quite fit; "we groan, longing to be clothed with our heavenly dwelling." But, oh, what a blessing are those groans! What a sweetness to feel homesick for heaven! What a glorious longing fills my heart to overflowing!

Wait a minute, Joni, perhaps you are thinking. *I'm not homesick for heaven. It's not like I'm absorbed by the things of earth, it's just heaven doesn't feel like my home yet.*

If this is you, don't panic. If, for you, heaven is still a glass house on some golden street rather than a warm and loving home, then hang in there. If you find it difficult to muster up longing for celestial mansions, don't worry.

It's more than that . . . much, much more.

FATHER CREATOR, THE WORLD you have made is so beautiful. Perfect snowflakes. Painted canyons. Sculpted mountain ranges. Sometimes such beauty makes it hard to muster up longing for celestial mansions. Give me a divine dissatisfaction with everything wonderful on earth so that I will truly be homesick for heaven. ✐

PART 6

HEAVEN HAS OUR HEART'S DESIRE

There is a heaven, for ever, day by day,
The upward longing of my soul doth tell me so.

— PAUL LAURENCE DUNBAR

Take a minute to consider a time when you were actually homesick. Not for heaven, but for your earthly home. Remember the aching? The sense of feeling like a stranger in your surroundings?

Boy, I remember it. I felt like my guts were being ripped out. I bawled when I was a little girl and had to stay at Aunt Dorothy's while my mother had a gallbladder operation. Then there was church camp. I was miserable. And that Thanksgiving when I first moved to California (of course, everyone first feels like a misfit in California).

My most recent bout with homesickness was in Bucharest, Romania. It was the middle of the night and I knew I was an alien as soon as I wheeled into the musty hotel lobby. A single dangling light bulb cast long shadows over dusty sofas and lamps leftover from the fifties. Prostitutes hid in a dark corner puffing cigarettes. From somewhere behind the desk, a radio featured Elvis Presley wailing "I Wanna Be Your Teddy Bear." There were bullet holes in the concrete wall. Moths and exhaust fumes filtered in through the open door, and somebody was screaming at a neighbor down the street.

I was tired, hungry, and dirty. There were no ramps for my wheelchair. I didn't fit in the bathroom. I didn't feel at home in the restaurant where they served tough meat swimming in oil and garlic. Everything about the place—the language, the culture, and especially the pillow on my mattress—made me long for Calabasas, California. It was awful. I know you've felt the same.

Why did Calabasas grip my heart? Was it the sidewalk ramps and curb-cuts? Radio stations playing better tunes than Elvis hits? Superior restaurants? Why do I feel I fit in California and not in Romania?

When you get homesick, your heart may tug for your own mattress and pillow, but this doesn't account for that gut-wrenching ache. Home must be more than the street address where you live. What makes home is not a place, but who lives there. You feel at home when your heart is nestled near the one you love.

Because home is where your heart is.

STILL NOT SATISFIED

I love you, O LORD, my strength. The LORD is my rock, my fortress and my deliverer; my God is my rock, in whom I take refuge. He is my shield and the horn of my salvation, my stronghold.

—Psalm 18:1-2

Sometimes, when you least expect it, even the people who make up home aren't enough. Sometimes when you're all tucked in with your own pillow and blanket, with the voice of the one you love close by, another kind of homesickness—a deeper kind—sneaks up on you.

Fragrant pine branches and the softness of falling snow. It was home at its 1957 best. Especially with a Christmas Eve visit from Uncle George and Aunt Kitty. Together, with the rest of the family in the candlelit living room, we sat on the couch and listened to Bing Crosby Christmas music on the radio. It was a quiet time. It was home.

Suddenly, out of nowhere, I was broadsided with homesickness. Good grief, there I was in the coziest of houses snug on the couch between people I loved, yet mantled with homesickness—a nostalgia for a bigger kind of home. I didn't catch on at first, but I was in the middle of another one of those heavenly longings.

The next morning that sensitive longing retired in the presence of mundane things, and I became my ordinary self. It was Christmas Day. I shelved my fascination with the strange longing and rushed headlong into my pile of presents. I ripped open the paper of one gift and asked, "Is there more?" And then another gift, asking, "How many left?" and then after the final present, whined, "Is that all there is?"

When it comes to heaven, we are all children opening a thousand beautiful Christmas presents and asking after each one, "Is that all there is?"

Maybe you're simply feeling awkward and uncomfortable in God's glittering, golden throne room. For that matter, you're still hung up in this tangle of earthly imagery whenever you picture heaven. You see yourself seated at the Wedding Feast of the Lamb where, presumably, there's no need for air-conditioning or central heating in the banquet hall. But where do you draw the line in dispensing with the paraphernalia of earth when picturing heaven? If the banquet is to be eaten decently, surely we will need knives and forks. Pots and pans to cook stuff in. Mixers must be somewhere in the background. And who does the dishes?

I can understand if these images don't make you yearn for your heavenly dwelling. It's not that you're absorbed by the things of earth; it's just that heaven doesn't *feel* like home. Yet the images painted in the Bible represent something designed to grip your heart, possess your soul, and call forth a powerful homesickness that makes you want to hurry up and unlock the front door of that mansion of yours.

Wouldn't it be nice to feel nostalgic for heaven that way?

WHAT DO YOU WANT?

Throwing his cloak aside, he jumped to his feet and came to Jesus. "What do you want me to do for you?" Jesus asked him. The blind man said, "Rabbi, I want to see."

—Mark 10:50-51

When it comes to heaven, why don't you make a Christmas list—all the best joys, gifts, and presents that you imagine heaven will offer. Ask your heart the question: What do you want? There's no restrictions on the list. The sky's the limit.

Now imagine getting it all. How soon do you think you would grow restless, before you'd say, "Is that all there is?"

Try another list, a deeper one. Endless talks with Beethoven about music or long chats with Mary Cassatt about Impressionism. How about a fit, healthy body for all you who have disabilities? Running? Dancing? A good conscience, freedom, peace of mind? It might be a few more thousand years before these would bore you, but eventually even they would become ho-hum. Is there *nothing* that will ultimately satisfy our hearts?

Thankfully, our hearts are always a beat ahead of our minds and bodies. Proverbs 4:23 is not off base when it says the heart goes deeper than the mind: "Above all else, guard your heart, for it is the wellspring of life." True, it also says the heart is desperately wicked, but that still demonstrates that it is the seat of deep passions. Important things happen in the heart. Out of it "flow the issues of life." We may have one foot here and the other in the hereafter, but our heart is often that part of us which tugs and pulls at that one foot stuck in the mud of earth, saying, "Get off of the earthly images, would you? Up here is what you're longing for."

Really? Does our heart have the answer? Can we trust our heart to *really* know what it wants?

When people approached Jesus with a need, it's curious that He often responded, "What do you want?" I've always thought this was an odd thing to say since, first, He could read their minds, and second, their need was often obvious—like Bartimaeus, the blind beggar, for one. But Jesus has His reasons for asking. He urges us to explore our heart's list of wants because He knows that we desire something deeper than getting a few surface needs satisfied.

And when it comes to heaven, He knows we desire something more fundamental than pleasure, prosperity, or power. Does our heart have something to say in response to this haunting echo?

Like tides on a crescent sea-beach,
　　When the moon is new and thin,
Into our hearts high yearnings
　　Come welling and surging in—
Come from the mystic ocean,
　　Whose rim no foot has trod—
Some of us call it Longing,
　　And others call it God.

— William Herbert Carruth

HEALING THAT OLD ACHE

*For where your treasure is, there your
heart will be also.*

—Luke 12:34

When it comes to attempting to heal that old ache, the human heart has had lots of experience. It does not really want to possess heaven so much as to be possessed by it. It desires not so much pleasure, for pleasure can be exhausted. Our heart wants something glorious that lasts.

What the heart desires is ecstasy.

Ecstasy is that marvelous euphoria in which we totally forget ourselves, and yet find ourselves. It is rapturous delight. Intense joy. Pure passion. When it comes to heaven, we want to be overpowered and caught up in something grand and wonderful outside ourselves. We want to be swept and wrapped up in a joy that weaves itself through every nerve and fiber. Like Elijah in his chariot, we want to be captured and carried away.

This is what our heart wants. This would be heaven without boredom.

Last night I experienced a taste of heaven when I wheeled out to my backyard to look at the full moon. It shone perfectly round and pale white through a sheer curtain of high, thin clouds. A sprinkle of blue stars peeked through the haze, and someone down the street was playing a Chopin melody on a piano.

For a split second I was in ecstasy. My heart broke for joy and then . . . it was gone. Whenever we stumble upon ecstasy, our heart knows beyond a doubt that this is *it*. It's a glorious healing of that old ache, even if but for a short moment.

Romantic love is as close as many people get to the healing of that ache. Trouble is, most people forget that romantic love is meant to point us to a greater, more fulfilling joy that enraptures. People cherish the glory they see in their lover, and they forget that the glory is not *in* the one they love, so much as shining *through* him or her. They don't realize that all the glory comes from beyond the one being cherished, like a light reflecting in a mirror. They make the mistake of idolizing the one by whom they are smitten, rather than reading the cues that keep whispering, "I'm only a reminder of something, Someone else. Quick, who do I remind you of? Here's a hint: I'm made in the image of God."

Most people never take this broad and glorious hint.

With Christians it is different. Christians get the hint, recognize the cues, and understand that the person we love is stamped with the image of God. We have the "homing detector," the flight instruments to help us see that the converging points in eternity *do not* meet in the face of the one we love, but pass through to meet in the face of God.

> **LORD, CAPTURE MY HEART** and carry me away with thoughts of heaven that can heal my deepest longings. Possess me so with heaven that my life and relationships with others reflects your power within. When trials and temptations come, catch me up in heaven's joy so that my decisions and choices will be yours. ✒

LOVE ONE ANOTHER DEEPLY

Now that you have purified yourselves
by obeying the truth so that you have
sincere love for your brothers, love one
another deeply, from the heart.

—*1 Peter 1:22*

To love each other deeply is to acknowledge that the divine glory that we see in the eyes of another *is* a reflection from beyond. This makes Christian love all the sweeter and each friend is an open invitation to see Jesus in him or her. What's more, the love Christians share lasts much longer than any old romance. It lasts longer than a lifetime.

Second, we have a built-in warning system that sounds an alarm if we start to idolize the one we love. God wants us to learn that human love is a signpost pointing to divine love. The one we love is a gift from God and, as a gift, points us to the Giver who is the One and only One who can provide an overflowing cup of joy, if not occasional ecstasy. This warning system keeps love, whether for our husband, wife, or friend, rightly focused and constantly refreshed.

Third, and most important, when we Christians love each other deeply, we catch a glimpse of that particular facet of God's love that is being cut, honed, and shaped in the life of the one we deeply love. We savor a foretaste of their true identity reserved in heaven, we inhale the fragrance of the heavenly person they are becoming. We see a particular aspect of heaven in them, we rejoice, and God receives glory—the mirror reflects His image back to Himself, and, once again, we are reminded that one day in eternity He shall indeed "be all and in all."

When I look into the eyes of a brother in Christ whom I love or a sister whom I cherish, I can almost see the spiritual being they are right behind their pupils. I also can't help but see their future divine fulfillment: "Christ in you the hope of glory." So you know what I do? In my mind, I get out my brush, mix some flesh tones, and I paint their face. I choose a certain color for the eyes, or I angle my brush for the slant of the cheek. Often I get so engrossed in the face, I forget what's being said. I hear the heavenly echo in his voice, the haunting in his eyes, and I just have to portray it. As I said in the first chapter, it is painters who most often try to capture the echo of heavenly music. And when I see that timeless look in someone's eyes, I head for that art easel in my imagination.

Within our heart we find a shadow of heaven, especially as we "love one another deeply," for love is an unconscious desire for heaven. We now know what we want. We know the answer to our heart's longing.

> I see Jesus in your eyes and it makes me love Him,
> I feel Jesus in your touch and I know He cares,
> I hear Jesus in your voice and it makes me listen.

> —Sharalee Lucas

IN THE HEART OF GOD

*My flesh and my heart may fail, but
God is the strength of my heart and my
portion forever.*

—*Psalm 73:26*

What you see reflected in the ones you love, is God. He and He alone provides the healing of that old ache. That's why heaven has to be more than a place. Much, much more.

It must be a Person.

Your primordial desire is that you want God more than anything else in the world. Like St. Augustine said, "Thou hast made us for thyself, and therefore our hearts are restless until they rest in thee."

Yes, your heart's home is in the heart of God. He has placed within you a yearning for Himself, a desire to know Him and understand what He is like. Pleasures and treasures on earth may be sought after and not found, but only God comes with the guarantee that He *will* be found. "'You will seek me and find me when you seek me with all your heart. I will be found by you,' declares the Lord, 'and will bring you back from captivity'" (Jeremiah 29:13–14). Hurrah, no more exile!

More specifically, He will be found in Jesus Christ. Jesus is the source of the haunting echo and the heavenly song. Jesus is

God wearing a human face. He is real and not abstract. Jesus is sunshine to our heart. Not just to our logic, but our heart. Praise God, we *know* the answer to our heart's longing. It's Jesus!

Our longings are satisfied in Him for "the Son is the radiance of God's glory and the exact representation of his being" (Hebrews 1:3). We can know God—our Father who art in heaven—if we know Jesus. And knowing Him, as we would desire to know a Lover, is ecstasy. His invitation to "enter into the joy of the Lord" is like stepping into a raft and being carried helplessly along a surging current, spilling over and splashing with joy. Please note that the joy of the Lord does not enter into us, but we, into it. We are enveloped by something larger, something greater than ourselves, a heavenly "in-loveness" in which we can do nothing but laugh and enjoy the ride. Jesus smiles, stretches out His hand and welcomes us into His raft with the invitation, "whoever loses his life for my sake will find it" (Matthew 10:39).

When you enter into the Lord's joy, ecstasy spills not only into laughter, but into song. A song, like poetry, is more the language of the heart than mere prose. This is why the old hymn writers who were ecstatic about God *always* sang about heaven.

Heaven is a place, and also a Person in whom I am lost in wonder, love, and praise. My heart insists that I sing when heaven courses through my veins.

> Changed from glory into glory,
>   Till in heav'n we take our place,
> Till we cast our crowns before Thee,
>   Lost in wonder, love and praise!
>
> —Charles Wesley

FACE TO FACE

*One thing I ask of the LORD, this is what
I seek: that I may dwell in the house of
the LORD all the days of my life, to gaze
upon the beauty of the LORD and to seek
him in his temple.*

—*Psalm 27:4*

Here's a pop quiz for all you romantics: in whose face do we find ecstasy lasting? Take a broad and glorious hint from Psalm 27:8: "My heart says of you, 'Seek his face!' Your face, Lord, I will seek." And if you need another reminder, listen to Psalm 105:4: "Look to the Lord and his strength; seek his face always." The points of eternity converge in the face of our Savior.

Since you got the answer to that question, this next one is easy: What are the correct coordinates for focusing your faith? The faith of which I have been speaking up until now is only the lens, the spectacles through which "the eyes of the heart may be enlightened" (Ephesians 1:18). The faith I've been describing is only a way of seeing and, therefore, believing something. But this isn't the whole story.

The correct coordinates on which to focus the eyes of the heart are Hebrews 12:2: "Let us fix our eyes on Jesus, the author and perfecter of our faith." Jesus is the Unseen Divine Reality. Everything shall find its future divine fulfillment in Him. "For no matter how many promises God has made, they are 'Yes' in Christ," says 2 Corinthians 1:20. This means *every* promise. The Author and Perfecter has conceived every unseen divine purpose and has planned its fulfillment to be a part of the wonder of heaven, "so that in everything he might have supremacy" (Colossians 1:18).

Everything from Pikes Peak to my backyard washed in the glow of a full moon—every bit of beauty here is but a shadow of something far more beautiful there—a longing to be clothed with the beauty its Designer originally intended.

Not only this dusty little planet will find fulfillment but, God willing, the teenager in the white-sequined dress will too. The Iranian gas station guys. And the little Asian girl in the Hair and Nail Shoppe. He will give us much more than the innocence we were groping for back in the Garden; He has imputed to us His righteousness. Our future divine fulfillment is alluded to in l John, for one day "we shall see Him and be like Him." Completely.

To pursue heaven is to pursue Him. To pursue Him is to find heaven.

It's that simple. If you wholeheartedly pursue Jesus, you can't help but be heaven-minded and sigh with Psalm 73:25: "Whom have I in heaven but you? And being with you, I desire nothing on earth."

> **LORD, I SEE YOU** in the faces of those I love. Help me pursue you and nurture my "romance" with you with as much (or more!) enthusiasm as I put into my relationships here on earth. ✒

ON THINGS ABOVE

Since, then, you have been raised with Christ, set your hearts on things above, where Christ is seated at the right hand of God.

—*Colossians 3:1*

When you consider that the first and greatest commandment is to love the Lord with all your *heart and mind,* it follows that we should set our *entire being* (that's what it means when it says "heart and mind") on things above.

My heart is the seat of all kinds of appetites and affections. Isn't yours? Our heart is hungry, not for food, but for a whole range of wrong coordinates. Sometimes the hunger in our heart gets us into trouble, and we wish we could curb the appetites.

God has good reasons for placing within us a heart that has such burgeoning appetites. He does so in order to test us and humble us, to see what is in our innermost being, to see whether or not we would follow Him. To see if we will zero in on the right coordinates. Will you succumb to the handsome face of your best friend's husband or will you choose heaven? Will you covet that third Penn International 50W fishing reel or will you desire heaven? Will you max out four credit cards on new wallpaper, carpet, and furnishings or will you invest in heaven?

To hunger is to be human, but to satiate yourself on God is to send your heart ahead to heaven. Feed on Him in your heart, and you will be yanking that foot out of the mud of earth and stepping closer to eternity. And where we place our citizenship, whether in heaven or on earth, is revealed by those things we passionately desire. If we desire dull, sensual things of earth, our souls reflect that dullness; if our desires rise to find fulfillment in the exalted, in the noble, pure, and praiseworthy, then and only then do we find satisfaction, rich and pleasurable.

The great in the kingdom of heaven will simply be those who set their heart on Christ and loved Him more. The great will be those who, having received a "You're off course!" warning from the heart's homing detector, simply got back on track.

That's the way I want to live. When I read, "Delight yourself in the Lord and he will give you the desires of your heart" (Psalm 37:4), I want to focus on Jesus, not my heart's list of desires. True contentment on earth means asking less of this life because more is coming in the next.

Because God has created the appetites in your heart, it stands to reason that He must be the consummation of that hunger. Yes, heaven will galvanize your heart if you focus your faith not on a place of glittery mansions, but on a Person, Jesus, who makes heaven a home.

WITH MY MIND SET on heaven, Lord, there is no place on earth that I can be that you are not there too. With my mind set on heaven I can endure through any circumstance. With my mind set on heaven I can love you more. Keep my mind on you . . . and heaven. 🖊

THINKING GOD'S THOUGHTS

> *"For my thoughts are not your thoughts, neither are your ways my ways," declares the LORD. "As the heavens are higher than the earth, so are my ways higher than your ways and my thoughts than your thoughts."*
>
> —Isaiah 55:8-9

After Bible study a few of the girls started talking as we sipped coffee. You'd think we would have discussed the apostle's encouragement to set our hearts and minds on things above, right? Wrong. Instead, we discussed the advantages of the stand-up toothpaste tube. We discussed the sale at the May Company, whether or not Excedrin PM is just a marketing ploy, and the latest reports of what the First Lady has been up to.

There's nothing wrong with these thoughts, but God's thoughts are higher than ours. I don't think God stays up at night wondering why they don't standardize electric plugs worldwide.

My thoughts need to rise to the heavenlies where Christ is seated. This means more than just thinking nice Girl Scout thoughts that are clean and reverent. "Set your minds on things above" means just that: thinking about things above.

This struck me not long ago when, during a visit to Italy, we explored Rome's Basilica. At the front of the cavernous cathedral, resplendent in Italian marble, mosaics, and statuary, was not the altar I expected to see. Instead, there was a large throne. It was fashioned from dark gold wood and surrounded by gilded clouds and bolts of lightning. It sounds gaudy, but actually, it was rather inspiring.

I thought about the throne in the Basilica as I laid in bed one night. I focused on the verse that says, "He sits on the throne of our praises." I decided to *think* about just that: A throne made of people's praises. Each joint and leg represented "Thou art worthy" or "You are holy" or "Your name is wonderful" and many more. I pictured God's delight in reclining on such praises. Not your garden-variety delight, but joy-filled laughter.

Is this all too heavenly minded? No way. When my mind chews on Scripture, as well as its symbols of heaven, faith has something to grow on.

To set our minds on Christ means not only the contemplation of the divine in heaven, but the divine on earth. Jesus has given us His thoughts and we have "the mind of Christ" when we lay hold of Him and His ideas. Picture Jesus blessing the little children. Think about Him tousling the hair of a little boy or taking in His hands the face of a child and blessing her. How noble, how lovely of Jesus. Think about Him reaching out to heal the bleeding hurt of a woman with a hemorrhage. How tender, how compassionate of Jesus. Think about Him turning a face of steel toward religious phonies and squaring off against sin. How holy and awesome of Jesus. And how changed you are after thinking such thoughts.

GOD AND HEAVEN

And God raised us up with Christ and seated us with him in the heavenly realms in Christ Jesus.

—Ephesians 2:6

To think about heaven is to think about Jesus. To pursue heaven with your heart is to pursue Him.

I'm not taking literary license. Heaven and God are intimately entwined, and the pursuit of one is the pursuit of the other. Matthew 23:22 says, "He who swears by heaven swears by God's throne and by the one who sits on it." Heaven is the place where God so much *is,* that you can refer to one or the other and virtually mean both.

The King of heaven wants us to see this tight connection between the Place and the Person. When our heart melts into God's and when our mind is thinking on Him, Place and Person no longer seem separated. "God [has] raised us up with Christ and seated us with him in the heavenly realms in Christ Jesus" (Ephesians 2:6). Amazing! When we understand our position in Christ, we begin to grasp our position in the heavenly realms. We are *already seated* with Christ in the heavenly realms. I'm not talking about astral projection or anything spooky. We're not actually in heaven the place, yet. But we *are* in the heavenly realms in that it's a sphere in which we live under God's rule and His Spirit's blessing. We are under the dominion of the King of heaven, and that places us in His realm. The King has come as well as His kingdom. The King is in our midst, and His kingdom is within us. All signs point to there *and* here. All signs lead to Him because all signs come from Him.

Use your eyes of faith here. This is another one of those unseen divine realities. God simply wants to get your mind racing and your heart beating with a present-tense excitement, a right-around-the-corner anticipation of heaven. Isn't that the way strangers on foreign soil are supposed to feel about their homeland?

Live in the present tense of heaven and you will smell the heavenly fragrance of the person you will become. Your life will have intensity and depth. You will sit close to self-scrutiny, understanding that by your words and actions you are doing earth a world of good. Your heaven-inspired faith will give you joy and peace, without parade or noise.

Most of all, you will feel at home. You will see "our Father who art in heaven" not as the Incomprehensible, but as Jesus sees Him: Abba-Father. Daddy. Home is where Daddy is.

> Heav'n above is softer blue,
>> Earth around is sweeter green!
> Something lives in every hue,
>> Christless eyes have never seen:
> Birds with gladder songs o'er-flow,
>> Flow'rs with deeper beauties shine,
> Since I know, as now I know,
>> I am His, and He is mine.
>> — George W. Robinson

I MISS MY HOME

But in keeping with his promise we are looking forward to a new heaven and a new earth, the home of righteousness.

—2 Peter 3:13

I like earth. But my heart pumps for heaven. Our hearts hold a shadow of heaven. Heaven is a place, and also a Person in whom I am lost in wonder, love, and praise.

Calabasas, California, is nice, but it pales in the light of the heavenly realms. Home is pretty good here, but my homing instincts often have me pulling up a chair on the front porch of my mansion to shade my eyes and scan "a land that stretches afar." I have a glorious homesickness for heaven, a penetrating and piercing ache. I'm a stranger in a strange land, a displaced person with a fervent and passionate pain that is, oh, so satisfying. The groans are a blessing. What a sweetness to feel homesick for heaven for "a longing fulfilled is sweet to the soul" (Proverbs 13:19).

Never was this symbolized more clearly than at one of our recent JAF Ministries' retreats I helped lead for families of disabled children. After a week of wheelchair hikes, Bible studies, and arts and crafts, I listened as the microphone was passed from family to family, each tearfully sharing how wonderful the time had been. Some talked of meeting new friends. Others, of the games, music, and hikes. A few said how they wished the week could go on and on.

Then little red-haired, freckle-faced Jeff raised his hand. He had Down's syndrome and had won the hearts of many adults at the retreat. People had been captivated by his winsome smile and joyful spirit. Everyone leaned forward to hear his words. Jeff grabbed the mike and kept it short and sweet as he bellowed: "Let's go home!" He smiled, bowed, and handed back the microphone. All the families roared with laughter.

His mother told me later that, even though Jeff thoroughly immersed himself in the week's festivities, he missed his daddy back home.

I identify with Jeff. The good things in this world are pleasant enough, but would we *really* wish for it to go on as it is? I don't think so. The nice things in this life are merely omens of even greater, more glorious things yet to come. God would not have us mistake this world for a permanent dwelling. It was C. S. Lewis who said something about not mistaking pleasant inns for home on our journey to heaven. I'm with him and I'm with Jeff. It's a good life, but I am looking forward to going home.

I miss my home.

I miss God.

FATHER, I MISS YOU. I miss a closeness to you that is tangible. I long for the righteousness of heaven. Focus my eyes of faith. Bring heaven forward into a vivid reality in my heart and mind that will spur me on to righteous living now. ✐

PART 7

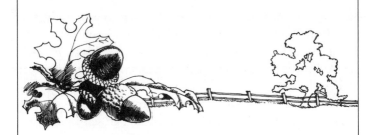

HEAVEN: THE HOME OF LOVE

> Heaven is the day of which grace is
> the dawn, the rich, ripe fruit of which
> grace is the lovely flower; the inner
> shrine of that most glorious temple to
> which grace forms the approach and
> outer court.
>
> — THOMAS GUTHRIE

She was just a little girl drawing water at a well outside the city walls
of Jerusalem when they met, and the smiles between them caught the
eyes of their parents. The years passed, their friendship grew, and it
wasn't long before the families of both Judith and Nathaniel were hap-

pily contemplating a wedding. The parents made the decision, while Judith and Nathaniel freely consented. That was the custom. That was the Jewish way.

However, it would be a long time before they would actually live together. In all probability, it would be an entire year before her groom would return for Judith and take her into his own house. She could hardly wait! The separation between them seemed endless.

One morning Judith woke up and realized a full year had almost passed. She knew Nathaniel could be coming for her at any time. She also knew he and his groomsmen would come for her at night. That was another custom. Which night? She had no idea and that made it all the more exhilarating.

One evening after dinner, as she was leaning on the window sill, Judith heard a faint voice in the distance, "The bridegroom is coming! He's coming!" This was it! The bridegroom was on his way! The bridesmaids caught wind of the warning and hurried to Judith's home to help her get dressed in her bridal garment. In a matter of moments, the torchlight processional halted outside her home.

When the bride, dressed in her gown, stepped through the door and onto the street, the wedding party cheered. Amidst singing and laughter, Nathaniel took Judith's hand and together, with the party, they walked by torchlight back to the home of Nathaniel's father. When they arrived at the house, Judith and Nathaniel greeted the guests and welcomed everyone to the wedding banquet.

There was dancing, music, and laughter up and down the street where Nathaniel lived. And, from that day on, Nathaniel and Judith lived happily ever after.

What glorious symbols for you and me as we wait for heaven!

BEHOLD THE BRIDEGROOM!

*After that, we who are still alive and are
left will be caught up together with them
in the clouds to meet the Lord in the air.
And so we will be with the Lord forever.*

—*1 Thessalonians 4:17*

John 3:29 tells me that "the bride belongs to the bridegroom."
I'm His possession. My life is hid with Christ in God, and who
I am won't appear until He appears. My life is wrapped up in
the One who redeemed me. Redeemed me in *love*. So, naturally
I'm going to pine for Him and feel homesick to be with Him.

My love for heaven is energized because I know how He feels
about me: "As a bridegroom rejoices over his bride, so will your
God rejoice over you" (Isaiah 62:5). Ponder that for a moment.
He *rejoices* over you, and don't say that word like a plaster-of-
paris saint in a less-than-amazing tone of voice. It's a jump-up-
and-down, clenched fist, throw-your-head-back, and yell out
loud, "Rejoice!" Jesus is brimming with heartfelt love for you
when He says in Song of Songs 2:14, "Show me your face, let me
hear your voice; for your voice is sweet, and your face is lovely."
This is a God in love.

It's not a matter of sweet words. No. He gave his life as His dowry, and the Cross shows me that He and His Father agreed on an exorbitant price. Every time I drink from the communion cup of wine, I remember the covenant between my Bridegroom and me. And I've promised Him I will drink from that cup in remembrance of Him until He comes.

Until He comes. That's the hard part.

Waiting is so hard. I sometimes find myself leaning on the edge of time's windowsill, wondering when, oh, when will He return? Jesus drops a hint in Revelation 16:15 when He says, "Behold, I come like a thief! Blessed is he who stays awake."

It makes me wonder about the rest of the marriage symbols between Judith and Nathaniel. What about the bride and His groomsmen waiting in the street? Is this a symbol of the Lord rapturing us from our homes and meeting us in the clouds? For "the dead in Christ will rise first. After that, we who are still alive and are left will be caught up together with them in the clouds to meet the Lord in the air" (1 Thessalonians 4:16–17). There are some who say that the Wedding Feast of the Lamb will be celebrated during the seven years of tribulation, and . . . after the seven years of tribulation, Christ will return with His bride to crush His enemies and set up housekeeping on earth. Is this the meaning behind these symbols?

I don't know. And I don't need to know. My responsibility as the betrothed is to be prepared and wait.

LORD, HELP ME AS I await your return to be more active in proclaiming your forgiveness and compassion to others around me. Show me how I can boldly invite those who as yet do not know you to the banquet being prepared in heaven. ✐

BE PREPARED

In righteousness I will see your face; when I awake, I will be satisfied with seeing your likeness.

—Psalm 17:15

I want to see the face of my Savior.

You may not realize it, but you do too. We find it hard to rest comfortably in a relationship—with God, with anyone—when we cannot see the face of the one we adore. The essence of who they are is held in the eyes, the mouth, the smile. The face is the focal point of personality.

When it comes to brides and bridegrooms, full intimacy comes between a man and a woman face-to-face. And when the Bible speaks of longing for God, it speaks in terms of wanting to see His face. The psalmist pleads with God, "Make your face shine upon us," and "Do not hide your face from us."

To hold the gaze of God is to find love, acceptance, and satisfaction.

Well, yes and no.

There is still a thick shield between God and us. When Moses pressed hard upon God to see His face, he would have been glad to use thick glass coated with UV block and grab a quick peek at

God through his fingers. But, no. Moses was only permitted to glimpse the backside of God's glory, for the Lord warned, "My face must not be seen" (Exodus 33:23). God didn't say this because there was nothing for Moses to see; He said it because He knew His light would kill. No man can see God and live. The Lord's glorious radiance would have snuffed Moses out in a nanosecond.

Even when Isaiah "saw" the Lord high and exalted on a throne, he did not behold God's face. He only glimpsed the periphery of the radiance of God. The sight threw Isaiah so deeply into despair over his sin that he cried, "Woe to me! . . . I am ruined! For I am a man of unclean lips" (Isaiah 6:5).

Sin is the problem. Sin is more than a thick shield between God and us. Acknowledging our stockpile of iniquities won't make it go away. No amount of confessing our sin will help us see God. That's backward. We don't have a clue as to the heinous nature of our sin until first we glimpse God's radiance, and then the words come tumbling out, "Woe is me!" The closer the apostle Paul got to God, the more he cried, "I am the chief of sinners." I used to think this was a pompous, grandstanding thing for Paul to say, but not any more. It's the cry of the saint sensitized to sin.

Our longing to see God is a longing, whether we know it or not, to see our sins exposed and to be cleansed by God Himself. Just as guilt will cause a child to hide in shame from her daddy's face, our deepest desire is to be clean, be free, to be transparent before the Father. And it won't happen until we see His face.

> Here, O my Lord, I see Thee face to face,
> Here would I touch and handle things unseen;
> Here grasp with firmer hand eternal grace,
> And all my weariness upon Thee lean.

> — Horatius Bonar

THE PURE AND SPOTLESS BRIDE

Everyone who has this hope in him purifies himself, just as he is pure.

—1 John 3:3

You and I going to heaven for a wedding? Our wedding? It's one thing to have funny feelings about a heavenly wedding, but I actually felt this way at my earthly wedding.

On the morning of the big day an usher brought word that the guests were seated, and it was time to line up. We reached the glass doors of the church, they swung open, and the blast from the organ gave us goose bumps.

Just before the wedding march, I glanced down at my gown. I had accidentally wheeled over the hem. It left a greasy tire mark. My bouquet of daisies were off-center on my lap since my paralyzed hand couldn't hold them. The dress just didn't fit. It was draped over a thin wire mesh covering my wheels, but it still hung clumped and uneven. My chair was spiffed up as much as possible, but it was still the big, clunky gray thing with belts, gears, and ball bearings that it always was. I was not the picture-perfect bride you see in magazines.

I inched my chair closer to the last pew to catch a glimpse of Ken at the front. He was craning his neck to look up the aisle.

He was looking for me. My face grew hot and my heart began to pound. Suddenly, everything was different. I had seen my beloved. How I looked no longer mattered. All that mattered was getting up to the front of the church to be with him. I *could* have felt ugly and unworthy, except that the love in Ken's face washed it all away. I was the pure and perfect bride. That's what he saw, and that's what changed me.

Years later, somewhere around our tenth wedding anniversary, I asked him, "What were you thinking on our wedding day?"

His answer delighted me. He said, "I woke up so early that morning, excited that I would see you in your wedding gown. I knew my eyes would be for you only. In fact, I'll never forget that wonderful feeling when I saw you wheeling down the aisle in your chair. You looked so beautiful."

"You mean, you didn't think much about my wheelchair? My paralysis?"

He thought for a minute, then shook his head. "No. Really, I just thought you were gorgeous."

Our entrance into heaven may be something like this. One day He will come for us and look into our eyes. We will hold His gaze. And all the stains and smears of sin will be purified out of us just by one searching of those eyes. One look from God will change us. And it will be more than we dreamed of.

> **LORD, I THANK YOU** for the thoughts of heaven and my reunion with you. Prepare my heart and mind as I wait for your coming that I may stand firm against sin. Help me to be a prepared bride, a pure and spotless bride, for you.

WISE AND FOOLISH VIRGINS

*Therefore keep watch, because you do
not know the day or the hour.*

—*Matthew 25:13*

We may be separated from our Savior, but that's no reason to sit around killing time until He comes. Jesus explains what brides ought to be doing while they're waiting for their groom:

> The kingdom of heaven will be like ten virgins who took their lamps and went out to meet the bridegroom. Five of them were foolish and five were wise. The foolish ones took their lamps but did not take any oil with them. The wise, however, took oil in jars along with their lamps. The bridegroom was a long time in coming, and they all became drowsy and fell asleep.
>
> At midnight the cry rang out: "Here's the bridegroom! Come out to meet him!"
>
> Then all the virgins woke up and trimmed their lamps. The foolish ones said to the wise, "Give us some of your oil; our lamps are going out."
>
> "No," they replied, "there may not be enough for both us and you. Instead, go to those who sell oil and buy some for yourselves."

But while they were on their way to buy the oil, the bridegroom arrived. The virgins who were ready went in with him to the wedding banquet. And the door was shut (Matthew 25:1–10).

Foolish virgins are those who think that the betrothal is just one big insurance policy guaranteeing them access to the Wedding without lifting a finger. Wise virgins understand that the betrothal carries with it big responsibilities. They act like they're married. They watch. They work. They stay awake. They don't sit around on their hands. In short, they act like they are loved and in love.

Before you rush to assume this means *doing* something, remember it means *being* someone. To wait is an occupation of the heart. To wait on the Lord is to love Him with spirited affection. With passionate delight. To wait on Him is to fix your eyes on those converging points in eternity: Jesus.

Thankfully, I've got some help with this thing about spiritual intimacy. My wheelchair. I get exhausted after a long day of sitting in my chair, and so most evenings I have to lie down at around 7:30. Lying in bed paralyzed, I have all the time in the world to wait on Jesus, to focus the eyes of my heart on those heavenly coordinates. No music. No TV. The clock ticks. If there's a breeze outside, the wind chimes tinkle. It's a place where I cannot *do* anything. I can only *be*. And I choose to be the wise virgin who pours my love into the marriage contract. I press my heart heavenward singing to the Lord a song just for His listening pleasure...

> O, this full and perfect peace!
> O, this transport all divine!
> In a love which cannot cease,
> I am His, and He is mine.
>
> —George W. Robinson

WAITING ON THE GROOM

*Wait for the LORD; be strong and take
heart and wait for the LORD.*

—*Psalm 27:14*

Most women I know are doing the second load of laundry at
7:30 p.m. or putting the third child to bed. Their healthy bodies are at work, while my paralyzed one is forced to rest. What
else is there for me to do but . . . wait?

Sometimes Ken gets concerned that I'm alone, or I should
say, choose to be alone. But he doesn't need to worry. Lying
there, looking at the ceiling, I squint my eyes of faith to focus on
unseen divine realities and their future fulfillments. I set my
heart and mind on heavenly glories above. I "taste and see that
the Lord is good" as I ingest favorite Scriptures (Psalm 34:8).

Within a short time, I'm in the heavenlies, picturing myself
kneeling on the throne room floor where Jesus is seated. Maybe
one evening I'll imagine I'm His handmaiden, at the foot of His
throne to serve. Another evening, His fellow intercessor kneeling next to Him. On another night, His sister. Sometimes His
child. If I'm under spiritual attack, I go to Him as the Captain
of the heavenly hosts.

When I relate to Him as the Lover of my soul, I'll quote out loud to the Lord a few verses from the Song of Songs. I'll tell Him He's the Rose of Sharon, the Lily of the Valley, the Fairest of Ten Thousand. "This is my lover, this is my friend, O daughters of Jerusalem. . . . He has taken me to the banquet hall and his banner over me is love . . . his left arm is under my head, and his right arm embraces me . . . strengthens me . . . refreshes me . . . for I am faint with love" (Song of Songs 2). And then, maybe I'll sing another hymn of love.

This intimate spiritual union is a two-way street. Occasionally, I'll picture Jesus whispering something to me that the Father said to Him in Isaiah 42:1: "Here is my servant, whom I uphold, my chosen one in whom I delight." Earth is one big premarital session for heaven, and although Jesus wants us to love Him passionately and single-heartedly, He more than matches it with love, pure and fervent.

On some evenings, He's the father running down the trail to embrace me, the prodigal, before I can speak a word of contrition. At other times, He is the mad farmer showering on me a full day's wage when I've hardly worked. On other evenings, He is the Master forgiving me, the sinful woman, before I realize I've done anything wrong. He's the king lavishing on me a banquet when I'm not even aware I'm malnourished.

It is "heaven" to know Jesus this way. And I mean that literally.

LORD JESUS, I'M WAITING. Waiting for your presence today. My eyes are fixed on you. My mind is meditating on your words. My heart is sensing your love. Fill me now with a fresh touch of your presence. I'm waiting. ✐

WHILE THE GROOM IS ABSENT

*This is eternal life: that they may know
you, the only true God, and Jesus Christ,
whom you have sent.*

—*John 17:3*

There are two kinds of knowledge. Just ask the wise and foolish virgins. If you asked a foolish virgin, "Do you know Jesus?" she would probably say, "Yes, I gave my heart to Him at a retreat in 1962, so I'm saved and going to heaven." She's reading a statement right off her insurance policy.

What would the wise virgin reply? "Yes, I know Jesus. I've given my life to Him, and I enjoy such wonderful intimacy with Him in prayer and studying His Word. Honestly, spending time with Him is the highlight of my day."

The apostle Paul knew Jesus and *knew* Jesus. He wrote in Philippians 3:8–9 of "the surpassing greatness of *knowing* Christ Jesus my Lord, for whose sake I have lost all things. I consider them rubbish, that I may gain Christ and be found in him, not having a righteousness of my own that comes from the law, but that which is through faith in Christ—the righteousness that comes from God and is by faith." Here Paul is talking about his position with God. He's talking about God doing something for him on His ledger, pronouncing, "You are forgiven." It's wonderful to have this kind of right standing, but there's more to knowing Christ than this.

Paul touches on this deeper knowledge in the next verse when he yearns, "I want to know Christ and the power of his resurrection and the fellowship of sharing in his sufferings" (Philippians 3:10).

Scholars explain that "to know" implies learning about someone through a deep, personal experience. It's the same sort of intimacy alluded to in Genesis where it says that Adam "knew" Eve. Theirs was a deep, personal experience. It is a physical illustration of the spiritual intimacy that God desires with us.

Right now, the bridegroom is absent. But, oh, I can hardly wait for the day when I break through to see the face of Jesus and once and for all *know* Him: To be overpowered, enraptured, and caught up in Someone grand and glorious beyond myself. To be swept and wrapped up in His joy. For time to stand still in a heavenly ecstasy in which I forget myself and yet find myself.

"As the deer pants for streams of water, so my soul pants for you, O God. My soul thirsts for God, for the living God. When can I go and meet with God?" (Psalm 42:1–2).

> Things that once were wild alarms
>   Cannot now disturb my rest;
> Closed in everlasting arms,
>   Pillowed on the loving breast.
> O, to lie forever here,
>   Doubt and care and self resign,
> While He whispers in my ear,
>   I am His, and He is mine.
>
> — George W. Robinson

THE WEDDING GIFT

And the ransomed of the LORD will return. They will enter Zion with singing; everlasting joy will crown their heads. Gladness and joy will overtake them, and sorrow and sighing will flee away.

—Isaiah 35:10

It's common practice for newlyweds to give gifts to each other. I suppose when I finally see my Savior, my gift to Him shall be whatever bits and pieces of earthly obedience I've done as evidence of my love. He said, "If anyone loves me, he will obey my teaching" (John 14:23), and I'm sure these bits and pieces will sparkle and shine like diamonds.

But what shall He give to us?

He will give the joy of heaven. To have my head crowned with everlasting joy is one of those earthly images that looks askew, but I don't mind. People caught up in ecstasy don't worry about such things. Suffice to say, it's a gift. A crowning gift.

Look at the gift with me for a moment. Joy is a fruit of the Spirit and that means it has in it the essence of eternity. When joy grips us, it always appears new, like a surprise. At the same moment, it seems ancient, as though it had always been there. Joy always has in it a timeless, eternal element. Pleasure and happiness may come and go, but joy seems to remain. Happy feelings have nothing of that air of eternity about them that joy has. That's because joy, in its essence, is of God. He is "the Lord of joy."

Whether experienced in shadow here or in light, there, joy is dynamic. It cannot stay stagnant or bottled up. Joy flows. Actually, it overflows. It floods back to God in gratitude, out to others like a fountain, and rushes through our own hearts in a torrent. This is why people weep for joy. We human beings, all finite and compacted, cannot contain the overflow. We are too small for how big joy is, and so we must weep. This also explains why joy breaks our heart. For like love, joy cannot be contained.

If you have experienced any of this, it's an inkling of the joy that will overtake us when we take just one glance at the Lord of joy. We will lose ourselves in Him. We will become one with Him. We will be "in Christ," we will have "put on Christ" at the deepest, most profound and exhilarating level.

This is why heaven is more than just a place of pleasure and happiness. The Lord's wedding gift to us will be the joy of sharing totally in His nature without us losing our identity. If we are to be praising God for all of eternity, which we shall be, then joy will be the dynamic. Thanks be to God for His indescribable gift!

LORD, I BRING TO you my bits and pieces of obedience as evidence of my love for you. And I thank you for the dynamic joy you give when I am obedient in even such small things. I praise you that heaven's greater, everlasting joy will be my gift one day. Hallelujah! ✎

The Bridegroom Cometh!

*My soul waits for the Lord more than
watchmen wait for the morning, more
than watchmen wait for the morning.*

—*Psalm 130:6*

Before we realize it, if we are blessed to be living at the time of
His return, we shall find ourselves in the embrace of our Savior
at the Wedding Supper of the Lamb. Heaven will have arrived.
The Lord's overcoming of the world will be a lifting of the curtain of our five senses. Life and immortality will no longer be
dim thoughts, but vivid and strikingly real.

Now, enjoy an unseen divine reality. Rev up your heart and
picture yourself taking a seat at the Wedding Supper. As you pull
up a chair to the banquet table, take a look at what's on the menu
from Isaiah 25:6: "On this mountain the Lord Almighty will
prepare a feast of rich food for all peoples, a banquet of aged
wine—the best of meats and the finest of wines."

There's no mistaking. This is a real banquet. They won't be
serving bologna or Spam. It will be "the best of meats." And the
beverage selection will not be Kool-Aid or cheap wine, but "aged
wine . . . the finest of wines."

I get a charge just thinking about it! I wonder who will sit
next to me, or across from me. I glance down the table and

there's my friend, Verna Estes, mother of seven, swapping baby stories with Susanna Wesley, mother of seventeen. There's Moses toasting Martin Luther. St. Augustine giving a bear hug to that jungle missionary who labored long and hard, unknown and unnoticed. At the other end of the table, Fanny Crosby is doing harmony on one of her hymns with the widow who faithfully played the rickety piano at the nursing home every Sunday. As for me, as soon as I see my friends who spent years getting me up in the morning, I jump up and grab a platter of meat. I just can't wait to serve them something.

Then I'll look up, and walking toward me will be Dad. And Mother. Before you know it, we'll break up into uncontrollable laughter. We will laugh and cry with a kind of tears that never flowed on earth. We will wipe our eyes and try to stop, then break up again, crying and laughing and pointing at everybody. "We're here! They are here! I knew it was true, but not this true!"

Christ will open our eyes to the great fountain of love in His heart for us, beyond all that we ever saw before. It will hit us that we, the church, are His bride. Not just individually, but together. United. One with each other, and one with Him. Suddenly, our joy is multiplied a millionfold.

Most poignantly, when we're finally able to stop laughing and crying, the Lord Jesus will really wipe away all our tears. And then, we join hands around the banquet table, and "in that day [we] will say, 'Surely this is our God; we trusted in him, and he saved us. This is the Lord, we trusted in him; let us rejoice and be glad in his salvation'" (Isaiah 25:9).

And the party is just beginning!

PART 8

AT HOME WITH OUR KING

In heaven, to be even the least is a
great thing, where all will be great;
for all shall be called the children
of God.

— THOMAS À KEMPIS

I'm thrilled that we will enjoy the Marriage Supper of the Lamb with its
feast of rich foods and the finest of wines, and we will delight in our
reunion with loved ones, and, yes, it will be exhilarating to reign over
angels and rule the earth with new bodies to boot. But I have to keep
remembering it will not be our celebration. It will be His.

We shall press in line with the great procession of the redeemed passing before the throne, an infinite cavalcade of nations and empires, age following age, Europe, Asia, Africa, North and South America, all standing shoulder to shoulder, the people of the islands of the seas in one happy parade, generations of the redeemed before the Cross and after, all bearing their diadems before God Almighty.

The judgment seat of Christ may have been center stage where Jesus showered praise on the believer, but all of heaven will turn the spotlight on the Lord to give Him back the glory. As Jesus rises from His throne before this great host, all crowns are lifted, all chimes ringing, and all hallelujahs hailing until the vocabulary of heavenly praise is exhausted. The universe will bow its knee and hail Jesus as King of Kings and Lord of Lords when He raises His sword in victory over death, the devil, disease, and destruction. We will press our crowns against our breasts, look at one another, and say, "Now?"

"Now!" all will shout. Together we will raise our voices, not in four-part harmony, but perhaps in twelve-part, with the twenty-four elders as "they lay their crowns before the throne" (Revelation 4:10–11) and sing:

> Holy, Holy, Holy! All the saints adore Thee,
>> Casting down their golden crowns around the glassy sea;
> Cherubim and Seraphim falling down before Thee,
>> Which wert and art and evermore shall be.

In a breathless moment—an infinite moment—we will comprehend that the whole plan of redemption was merely the Father's way of securing for His Son . . . a Bride . . . a Family . . . an Army . . . an Inheritance.

I could never dare keep those crowns for myself. Could you?

CROWN JEWELS

*They will sparkle in his land like jewels
in a crown. How attractive and beautiful they will be!*

—*Zechariah 9:16–17*

The party is just beginning. It will be Christ's coronation day.

If, indeed, we are given literal crowns, make no mistake about it—the diadems will be His. But the crowning purpose of God's plan will be to secure for the Son a grand chorus of Eternal Worshipers. This is what I was made for. This is the answer to all the times I asked on earth, "Why has God chosen me? Why not someone else?" The response is simply, *I am the Father's gift to the Son.* Ephesians 1:11–12 will then make perfect sense for "in him we were chosen in order that we might be for the praise of his glory." I will be the flashing and iridescent gift for the Son whom Zechariah admired.

Earth was one big diamond mine in which I was chiseled from the dirt, cleaned, polished, and fitted for a King's crown. Can you now understand why I want to win as many crowns as possible while on earth? True, greater rewards will enhance my service in heaven, but they will also magnify the glory Jesus will receive. The more crowns, the merrier God's praise. My motive in gathering a truckload of diadems is not to hoard them, but to have more to cast at Jesus' feet.

You and I were chosen to praise Him. It's that simple. What a shame that on earth we made it so complicated.

In the early days of my paralysis when I first learned about heaven, I zeroed in on it because it was the place where I would receive new hands and feet. Heaven was the place I'd be freed from the pain, and so, it became an escape from reality. A psychological crutch. At times, heaven was so me-centered that I felt as though the whole point of it was to get back all it owed me, all I had lost. And so, heaven became a death wish.

Time passed, and gradually it dawned on me that the Day of Christ would be just that—the Day of Christ, not the day of Joni. Glorified hands and feet and reunions with loved ones began to look more like fringe benefits to simply being on the invitation list to the coronation party. It will be Jesus' Day.

The privilege of casting your crowns at the feet of Jesus will be enough of an honor. Ruling the earth and reigning over angels, becoming pillars in God's temple and co-heirs of heaven and earth are almost incidental. What we become, receive, and do in heaven won't be the highlight of heaven. To be there and to *be to the praise of His glory* will be enough.

I *like* the idea of being a jeweled gift for Jesus:

When He cometh, when He cometh to make up His jewels,
All His jewels, precious jewels, His loved and His own:
    Like the stars of the morning,
    His bright crown adorning,
They shall shine in their beauty—Bright gems for His
    crown.

—William O. Cushing

CHRIST'S CORONATION DAY

The twenty-four elders fall down before him who sits on the throne, and worship him who lives for ever and ever. They lay their crowns before the throne and say: "You are worthy, our Lord and God, to receive glory and honor and power."

—Revelation 4:10-11a

If only we had stopped and read—really read—that "the God who made the world and everything in it is the Lord of heaven and earth" (Acts 17:24). It takes heaven to force us to fully comprehend what should have been plain on earth all along: Jesus is the Lord of heaven and earth.

We said it in our prayers, we sang it in our songs. But it never really clicked for us. That's because "us" kept getting in the way. All those years when earthly trials hit hard, we burnt rubber in our brains trying to figure out what it meant to us. How Jesus could be conformed in us. Everything was always "for us." Even Sunday worship service focused on how we felt, what we learned, and if the hymns were to our liking.

Why didn't we appreciate that God gave every trial, heartache, and happiness to show us something about Himself?

That we might appreciate His grace?

That we were being polished for the praise of His glory?

We always marvel that God shows an interest in us, but in heaven it will be clear that every earthy thing happened so that we'd show an interest in Him. In every trial, happiness, and heartache, God wanted us to think about Him.

While on earth, you never could have convinced us. We behaved like His will was done on-earth-as-it-is-in-heaven mainly to benefit our jobs and relationships. And whenever we talked about heaven, it was more along the lines of an eternal playground where we would receive lots of new toys while God, like a granddaddy, would nod and smile to see us enjoying ourselves.

What a shame that on earth we acted as though we did God a big favor by accepting Jesus as Savior. We pitied Jesus because His reputation could never quite be vindicated. We felt sorry for God because it seemed like His justice was never quite served; in fact, at times we were embarrassed for our "King" as we scrambled to defend Him over earthly holocausts and horrors. Jesus never appeared to flex his kingly muscles, and thus never got credit, much less glory.

We weren't the only shortsighted ones. Even the disciples had a small-minded view of God. They too failed to recognize the King in their midst. Occasionally the fog lifted from their thinking, and once, toward the end of Jesus' ministry, they rose to a heavenly perspective of their King and said, "Now we can see that you know all things." For a brief moment, their focus was off the kingdom on earth and fixed on the kingdom in heaven. It was a rare flash of revelation, and Jesus was moved enough to exclaim, "You believe at last!" (John 16:30–31).

Those words of Christ's rip at my heart. All Jesus wanted from us was, at last, to believe. We should have known it all along.

Against All Odds

And being found in appearance as a man, he humbled himself and became obedient to death—even death on a cross! Therefore God exalted him to the highest place and gave him the name that is above every name, that at the name of Jesus every knee should bow.

—*Philippians 2:8-10a*

Why were our times of drastic obedience and absolute trust only flashes, brief moments of illumination? Why did we always have such a hard time acting like Jesus was King?

Perhaps because on earth, He never acted like a king.

Or at least not like one would think a king should act. Jesus, however, had a good reason for cloaking His majesty under the robe of weakness, shame, and humility. It has to do with His glory in heaven. When the Father designed the plan of salvation, He initiated a scheme that would ultimately bring the highest and brightest glory to His Son, the King of the Cosmos. It was a plot that almost reads like an adventure story.

The plan was put into effect when the evil villain, Lucifer, enslaved the citizens of the kingdom of earth through treachery and deceit. He usurped the authority of the rightful Ruler and set up his own rival government. The good Ruler sent His most skilled servants to try to recapture the occupied territory, but with few exceptions, the villain seduced and defeated them. Finally, the Ruler sent His only Son, the rightful Prince, to invade Lucifer's territory, free the captive subjects, and retake the kingdom under the family banner.

But the battle tactics of the Son were odd, to say the least. In fact, the manner in which He fought seemed to insure defeat. At one point, when Lucifer had the Prince pinned, the Son merely yielded to the deathblow. All appeared lost and the people's hearts fainted in despair. Little did they realize the best and final part of the plan was just about to go into play. It was called the Resurrection, and it was the only battle tactic that could deliver the killing blow to the enemy and his hordes of evil rulers.

Now any struggle between a hero and the bad guys is interesting enough, but when the hero is disadvantaged, a new element is introduced. Now the hero is in far more danger and he appears to have less chance of winning. But if in his weakness he overcomes against all odds, he ends up twice as much the hero. When weak heroes outmaneuver strong villains, the victory is awe-inspiring.

And so, the Prince of Peace, the Lamb who let Himself be slain, will be glorified, not because He employed brute force against Satan, but because He didn't.

> **LORD, WHY DO I** have such a hard time acting like you are King? Is it because your battle tactics seems to throw me at the mercy of the devil? Yet you have assured me the victory is yours. Show me the areas in my life that still need to yield to you as my King. ✐

THE KING WHO WON
THROUGH WEAKNESS

And having disarmed the powers and authorities, he made a public spectacle of them, triumphing over them by the cross.

—*Colossians 2: 15*

My husband Ken tells me that judo has its uses. It's the art of using the power of your enemy to defeat him. The secret is simply to wait for that moment when the opponent's full strength can be used to defeat him. When my husband is attacked, he simply judos his assailant and sends the guy flying over his shoulder.

Jesus appeared passive and weak. We kept hoping He would behave as a monarch should and make the lives of His subjects happy, healthy, and free from trouble. But Jesus had other plans for earth. He kept doing judo. Especially against the devil. And most specifically at the Cross. At the exact moment the devil thought he had Christ cornered and pinned down in defeat, he unleashed his full satanic fury to finish Him off. But it was Christ's weakness and vulnerability that enabled Him to judo Satan into slitting his own throat.

Something glorious happened when the world's worst murder became the world's only salvation. When the cross, a symbol of torture, became a symbol of life and hope, it meant triple the glory.

Jesus ends up triple the hero in heaven because He won using weapons of warfare that were spiritual, and not carnal. His triumph was assured using divine judo. He won using perfect timing and patience. He won through waiting, yielding, and submission.

If we pitied Christ on earth or felt badly that His justice seemed aborted, we wasted our time. Jesus *did* flex His muscles as King on earth; our unskilled eyes, hearts, and minds just weren't trained to see it. He wore a crown; it just wasn't the crown we expected. Not one of gold, but of thorns.

Up in heaven, we may be tempted to smack our foreheads and exclaim, "How did we miss it?" But there will be no room for remorse. Our King of Kings will be too gracious to permit us such regrets. It will be obvious why His medals of monarchy were hidden. It was all engineered to help us exercise faith, develop trust, and demonstrate obedience, as well as to teach us timing and patience, waiting and yielding. The King overcame the Cross so that we might have power to parlay a bullying devil and thus accept our thorns, share our burdens, and carry our own crosses, while all the time turning tragedy into triumph and heartaches into victories.

With good grace, Jesus will not scold us for being so us-centered. He will assure us He knew our frame and remembered that we were but dust.

And *that,* dear friends, will compel us to love, praise, and rejoice in Him all the more. At that point, God's glory in heaven will open up exponentially to the hundredth power. His reputation will be vindicated. He will receive all the credit due Him, plus triple the glory. He will show Himself as He is, no longer the weak and suffering servant, but the mighty Sovereign of time and space.

THE GREAT AND TERRIBLE DAY

*For with fire and with his sword the
LORD will execute judgment upon all
men, and many will be those slain by the
LORD.*

—*Isaiah 66:16*

All this stuff about weakness and humility grates on the nerves of some people. They don't buy a God who would let Himself be mocked, kicked, and spit upon, all for the sake of justice. Especially justice on their behalf. How dare this weak, powerless God assert they need to be saved—and from their sin, no less!

On earth, they pushed their own kind of justice. And first on their agenda was to defame and defrock Jesus. Setting themselves up at the center of their own moral universe, they thought they had the power to put God on trial. They arraigned and indicted Him, accused and banished Him as some impotent third-rate deity. They kicked Him out of school classrooms and erased His mark from the public square. Profaning His name, they neutered God and tamed Him so He would bless their lusts and passions.

But in heaven, the record will be set straight. God will vindicate His holy name and dispense His pure and perfect justice. For a great many people, it will be terrifying.

What a shock when they behold this Jesus whom they tried to shove back into a Sunday school room. Horror will strike their hearts as the scene in Revelation 19:11–13 unfolds:

> I saw heaven standing open and there before me was a white horse, whose rider is called Faithful and True. With justice he judges and makes war. His eyes are like blazing fire, and on his head are many crowns. He has a name written on him that no one knows but he himself. He is dressed in a robe dipped in blood, and his name is the Word of God.

The same mouth that spoke peace and reconciliation will one day emit the sharp sword of judgment. Eyes like blazing fire? A robe dipped in blood? This is no senile Benevolence that drowsily wished human beings well while they were on earth, a God to be pitied or felt sorry for. This is the great and terrible Lord, the consuming fire Himself.

This is not a pretty sight for "it is a dreadful thing to fall into the hands of the living God" (Hebrews 10:31). The same eyes that glowed with compassion will one day blaze with fire. Is this the Rose of Sharon, the Lily of the Valley, my Bridegroom? Yes, this same Jesus, into whose loving hands I first fell, is the dreadful living God.

Lover and Avenger? He is perfectly one and the same. He is altogether loving in His justice, and just in His love. And because He is perfect, His justice is pure.

FATHER, I TREMBLE FOR the people of the world on the final judgment day. Your gentle compassion will turn to a blazing fire of consuming wrath. Yet at the same time I rejoice that you will bring about justice . . . a justice that extends to all . . . a perfect, pure justice for me. 🖋

HOW WILL THAT DAY FEEL?

*It is a dreadful thing to fall into the
hands of the living God.*

—*Hebrews 10:31*

Once in heaven, we will know in every fiber of our being, beyond a shadow of a doubt that whatever the Judge declares about us is true. As He says we are, so are we. No more, no less. Maybe we will even realize, in a dim, hazy way, this was our actual deep-down self on earth all along. If the Judge rules we were righteous in Christ, then "Hallelujah! I knew it all along." If He declares us unrighteous, wicked, and steeped in selfishness, then "curse me! I knew it all along." The self-evident truth about you or me will be clear to everyone.

That's why, as uncanny as it seems to us now, we won't cringe or cower on the great and terrible day of the Lord. Oddly, we will rejoice. This sounds insane because our human sense of compassion abhors the idea of justice being executed with unbridled sound and fury. On earth, justice is served as prisoners are quietly escorted from death row to chambers where hushed groups of people sit behind soundproofed windows and, without emotion, watch death happen.

But not in heaven.

There, judgment is full of emotion.

Smack-dab in the middle of the apocalypse, as bowls of wrath are being poured out with smoke and fire, we are found singing and rejoicing while watching the Judgment. This parenthesis of incredible praise is squeezed between the rage of God in Revelation 18 and what looks like Armageddon at the end of Revelation 19. In the mighty praise chorus of verses 1–10, we are numbered among the angels, the elders, and "the roar of a great multitude in heaven shouting: 'Hallelujah! Salvation and glory and power belong to our God, *for true and just are his judgments.*'"

Why will we happily agree with Jesus as He treads the winepress of the fury of the wrath of God Almighty? Will it be because the tables will finally turn on the bad guys? No. We will accompany the Judgment with choruses of praise because we will love purity and hate the perniciousness of evil. We will desire truth deeply and despise lies and wickedness. With perfect minds and devout hearts, we will joyfully accent all of God's judgments with a hearty "Yes!" And we'll do it as He's treading His grapes of wrath.

The Day of Christ will be a great and terrible day. Great for the righteous and terrible for the unrighteous.

FATHER, YOU ARE A just judge. If you were to judge my life apart from Christ, my destiny would be eternity spent without you. There is nothing good in myself except what your son has done. In this fact I rejoice, for I know that because of Christ, and his blood shed for me, you will declare me righteous. Thank you for that glorious hope. ✒

THERE IS A HELL

*Then death and Hades were thrown
into the lake of fire. The lake of fire is
the second death. If anyone's name was
not found written in the book of life, he
was thrown into the lake of fire.*

—*Revelation 20:14-15*

Yes, there is a hell.

It's unthinkable to talk about heaven without at least mentioning hell. Please note I didn't refer to it as "heaven's counterpart." Heaven has no counterpart. It has no opposite. Just as Satan is not God's opposite (for the devil is merely a created being—and a fallen one, at that!), neither does heaven have an opposite. In the vastness of God's infinite, as well as cleansed and purified universe, hell may end up being only a speck. A trash heap. A garbage dump.

Outside of Jerusalem, the holy city, there was a junkyard where the Jews took their garbage to burn. God's people thought it only a place fit to set fire to their waste. They ended up calling it Gehenna, and that became the biblical term for hell.

The actual hell will be the trash compactor of the universe. Hell will not pollute the purified universe, nor will it be a festering boil in the side of the new heavens, an ugly sore spot that forever seeps and demands somebody's attention. It may well be too small for that. I don't mean hell will be smaller than heaven in terms of population statistics, but in terms of its importance in the new heavens and new earth. Nobody pays much attention to smoldering junk heaps.

Jesus' teaching about hell with its wormwood and gall is meant to strike terror in our hearts, warning us that if heaven is better than we could dream, so hell will be worse than we can imagine.

Hell warns us to seek heaven. It is its own best deterrent.

I know this firsthand. At the time of my injury, doctors pumped me up with powerful drugs to get rid of the infection that was raging through my paralyzed limbs. My body was on fire with pain. When nurses turned me facedown on the Stryker frame, I could only see the floor and people's feet. Horrified, I saw the ugly cloven hooves of demons where there should have been shoes of nurses. The feet of friends were webbed with claws. I screamed at the nurses not to flip me face up, fearful that I would see ugly monsters. But when they turned me over, I was shocked to find everything normal.

What a hell. Looking back, I know my terror was drug-induced. But those frightening images remained with me even through subsequent years of backsliding and bitterness. In fact, during those years when I teetered on the brink of rejecting Christ entirely, scary cloven hooves would flash in my mind. For me, it was a warning: Hell exists; it's horrible, you don't want to go there, and you want to do everything in your power to keep others from choosing it.

FOR THE SAINT, HEAVEN is God. For the wicked, hell is God. Cursed are the impure in heart for they too shall see God! ✐

— Jonathan Edwards

SOME HAVE CHOSEN HELL

*Out of his mouth comes a sharp sword
with which to strike down the nations.
"He will rule them with an iron
scepter." He treads the winepress of the
fury of the wrath of God Almighty.*

—*Revelation 19:15*

No doubt about it. The world, for the most part, chooses the path to hell. Not many choose Christ and His heaven. For all the people who insisted "My will be done!" God will not dissuade. He will no longer strive with them, either by pointing to His glory in creation or by preaching to them from the Gospel. For those who turn their backs on Christ, there is no heaven.

Does this seem unfair? Does it seem cruel that unbelievers "will be thrown outside, into the darkness, where there will be weeping and gnashing of teeth" (Matthew 8:12)? Our human sense of justice may think so, but remember, God owes this utterly rebellious planet absolutely nothing. Were it not for God's quickening grace, we would all remain dead in our trespasses. Plus, were it not for His grace, this planet would have ripped itself apart at the seams long ago in hatred and violence.

That the human race has survived this long is a demonstration of God's compassion. The question is not "How could God let so many people go to hell?" but should be "How could God be so generous and save as many as He does?"

Human fairness is not the point, the justice of God is. If there's no judgment and subsequent hell, then it makes more sense to eat, drink, and be merry for tomorrow we die and . . . period. Nothingness. It's all over. But there *is* a hell. As well as a Judgment. "I saw the dead, great and small, standing before the throne, and books were opened. Another book was opened, which is the Book of Life. The dead were judged *according to what they had done*. . . . If anyone's name was not found written in the book of life, he was thrown into the lake of fire" (Revelation 20:12, 15).

That's the one verse in the Bible that makes my hair stand on end. Apocalyptic verses about signs of the times, earthquakes, floods, and pestilence don't do it. Not even word pictures about snarling beasts and ten-horned creatures or the heavens rolling up as a scroll and the mountains fleeing into the ocean. The worst verse in the Bible is the one about dead people being judged. That's because some of those dead will be my neighbor down the street, my elementary school teacher, the lady at the dry cleaners, or even those Muslim young men who work at the Shell gas station near my house.

When I pray, "Come quickly, Lord Jesus," I utter that word "quickly" with caution. Do I really want Jesus to return soon?

> **LORD, IF JUDGMENT WERE** up to me terrorists, drug dealers and child pornographers would feel your swift divine wrath right now. Yet you have promised you will judge the wicked. Until then, remind me to pray for them that you will bring such evil people to repentance and turn their hearts to you. Show me how I can be a means to help them choose you. ✐

DELAYING GOD'S WRATH

> *"He has sent me to proclaim freedom for the prisoners and recovery of sight for the blind, to release the oppressed, to proclaim the year of the Lord's favor." Then he rolled up the scroll, gave it back to the attendant and sat down.*
>
> —Luke 4:18b-20a

No one was sure how long He'd been gone. Rumor had it that one morning Jesus just hung up His carpenter's apron and headed off to the Jordan River to find the Baptist. Then something strange happened. When Jesus was baptized there was a thunderous voice, followed by a dove. Next, He vanished. Some say Jesus headed off into the wilderness. Others reported His whereabouts later on in Capernaum. That's when rumors really got weird. Sick people getting healed? Something about water becoming wine?

And now He was back in Nazareth.

The air in the synagogue was hot and tight. The attendant handed Jesus the scroll of Isaiah. He quietly unrolled it, found the verse He was looking for, and began to speak with the voice of uncommon authority: "The Spirit of the Lord is on me, because he has anointed me to preach good news to the poor.

He has sent me to proclaim freedom for the prisoners and recovery of sight for the blind, to release the oppressed, to proclaim the year of the Lord's favor" (Luke 4:18–19).

He stopped in the middle of the verse. Just like that, Jesus left it unfinished and sat down. The eyes of everyone were fastened on Him. Little wonder, they had never heard Isaiah 61 read in such a way, like the words were His own. Finally Jesus broke the silence, "Today this Scripture is fulfilled in your hearing." This threw everybody into confusion.

Perhaps it wasn't so much what He said, as what He didn't say. Jesus did not read the entire verse from Isaiah 61. He announced He had come to proclaim the year of the Lord's favor, but He failed to finish the sentence. He did not say what the people were hoping He would say: That He had come "to proclaim the day of vengeance of our God." It was obvious to the people gathered in that synagogue that Jesus had no intention of executing the wrath of God upon their Roman oppressors.

He left off the most terrifying part of the second verse of Isaiah 61 because He did not come to condemn or destroy. He came to seek and save the lost.

Jesus made it clear that His agenda was not to execute the wrath of God, but to bear in His own body that same wrath. I'm heartbroken by that statement: Jesus, precious Savior, did not come to execute the wrath of God, but to *bear in His own body* God's fury. All of the Father's white-hot anger against my sin was poured out on the cross. Because of Jesus, the Father has no anger left for you and me.

> **THANK YOU, FATHER,** for sending your son Jesus to die on the cross for my sin. Help me to be a witness of the power of the cross to those around me so that they will not end up getting trampled in the grapes of your divine wrath. ✒

GOD'S TIMING IS PERFECT

*He said to them: "It is not for you to know
the times or dates the Father has set by his
own authority. But you will receive power
when the Holy Spirit comes on you; and
you will be my witnesses in Jerusalem, and
in all Judea and Samaria, and to the ends
of the earth."*

—*Acts 1:7-8*

One day Jesus is going to return and finish the verse from Isaiah 61. He will judge the living and the dead. He will crush the wicked. Punish rebellious, impudent evildoers. He will upset nations and overthrow kings and rulers. He will institute the day of vengeance of our God.

I need to remember that God's timing is perfect. You and I have a job to do, just as the disciples were reminded when they asked Jesus when He would come back.

I need not bother myself with God's timing. I simply need to be bothered enough to witness. This is what tempers my pleas for the soon return of Christ. While Christ is in heaven, He is proclaiming through us the year of the Lord's favor, He is carrying out His agenda of compassion and forgiveness through you and me. He is still the tender, merciful Shepherd looking for more people to rescue, searching for lost men and women on whom He can gladly bestow salvation.

So when I begin to lean on the windowsill of eternity and pine for my Savior to fulfill His promise to return, I bite my lip and recall 2 Peter 3:9: "The Lord is not slow in keeping his promise, as some understand slowness. He is patient with you, not wanting anyone to perish, but everyone to come to repentance." That's all the reminder I need to get away from that windowsill and go rescue the perishing.

How patient of the Lord to hold His breath for virtually two thousand years before bringing down His vengeance. I don't mind the slowness of God even if it means having to spend extra years in this wheelchair. God's slowness means more time and opportunity to increase heaven's numbers. More time for His Inheritance to be enriched, His Body to be made complete, His Bride to be more beautiful, His Army to be greater in rank, and the grand chorus of Eternal Worshipers to be louder and more thunderous in their praise. In short, it means more glory for Him.

I can sum up 2 Peter 3:9 with this paraphrase: "The Lord is not slow in finishing His sentences, as some understand slowness. He is holding off the last part of Isaiah 61:2 so that, heaven willing, my neighbor, my relatives, and the people who work in my community will come to repentance."

Oh, how gracious of Jesus, how patient. How kind of our God, how merciful. Until the King of Kings and Lord of Lords returns with eyes of blazing fire, robe of blood, and sword and fury, you and I better get out there and proclaim the year of the Lord's favor.

CROWN HIM WITH MANY CROWNS

*His eyes are like blazing fire, and on his head are
many crowns. He has a name written on him that
no one knows but he himself. He is dressed in a robe
dipped in blood, and his name is the Word of God.*

—Revelation 19:12-13

The day dawned quietly over Nazareth, except for the crowing
of a rooster and barking from a few dogs. The hour was still early
but the sun was high, the air dry and hot. Any other morning the
streets of Nazareth would have been bustling with hawking vendors and women chatting on their way to the well. But this was
no ordinary day. This was the Sabbath. And this was no ordinary Sabbath. Jesus was in the synagogue.

Luke 4 records the crowd started demanding tricks, a magic
show, shouting, "Do here in your hometown what we have heard
that you did in Capernaum!" Jesus reminded them that crowds
demanded the same performance from Elijah and Elisha, but
like the prophets of old, He would do no miracles among faithless, stiff-necked, prideful people. He made clear His motives
and intentions. He had come for heaven's sake. This threw everybody into confusion. A scuffle broke out and then a town riot.
They drove Jesus out of the village and took him to the brow of

the hill to throw Him down the cliff. The story abruptly ends there, with Jesus escaping and going on His way.

From the very moment He embarked on His earthly mission He made it clear—He had come for heaven's sake. But wasn't the crowd satisfied with His mission statement?

The people wanted Jesus on their own terms, not His. But we can learn from their mistakes. We can see that everything happened so that we might show an interest in Him. And one day we will finally be convinced that the One whom we lauded with our lips as King truly did have supremacy in all things.

His kingdom came. *His* will was done on earth as it is in heaven. *His* word went forth and accomplished His purposes. *He* was sovereign Lord over all.

Is your blood pressure a notch higher like mine right now? Maybe you are feeling like me-awash in delight, yet reverent in fear. Tingling with joy, yet trembling with holy respect. Our God is an awesome God. I wish we were standing together underneath a starry dome, feeling small and swallowed up, and tuning into the faint and haunting melody of a hymn. A certain hymn striking a resonant chord in our souls.

It would be a moment of great happiness and wisdom. But this time, we wouldn't let it go. Nothing mundane or ordinary could drown it out, and we'd not only hold ourselves in that ecstatic state of listening to heaven's music, but we would lift our voices and sing along.

> Crown Him the Lord of heav'n:
>> One with the Father known,
> One with the Spirit through Him giv'n
>> From yonder glorious throne.

> —Matthew Bridges

PART 9

Getting Ready for Heaven

I would not give one moment of heaven for all the joy and riches of the world, even if it lasted for thousands and thousands of years.

— Martin Luther

My face flushed and my eyes became damp. For the fourth time that day, I needed to be lifted out of my wheelchair and laid down. I had to undress to readjust my corset—shallow breathing, sweating, and a sky-rocketing blood pressure were signaling that something was either pinching, bruising, or sticking my paralyzed body. My secretary tissued away my tears and unfolded my office sofa bed.

As she shifted my body, examining my legs and hips for any telltale pressure marks or red areas, I stared vacantly at the ceiling. "I want to quit this," I mumbled.

We couldn't find anything wrong. She put my clothes back on, hoisted me into my chair, and stepped back.

I looked sheepish. "Where do I go to resign from this stupid paralysis?"

Francie shook her head and grinned. She's heard me say it scores of times. My disability is, at times, a pain.

As she gathered the pile of letters off my desk, and was about to leave, she paused and leaned against the door. "I bet you can't wait for heaven. You know, like Paul said, 'We groan, longing to be clothed with a heavenly dwelling.'"

My eyes dampened again, but this time they were tears of relief and hope. "Yeah, it'll be great."

I sat and dreamed what I've dreamed of a thousand times: the hope of heaven. I jerked my will right side up, refocused my emotions, and realigned my thoughts. I mentally rehearsed a flood of other promises and fixed the eyes of my heart on unseen divine realities and future divine fulfillments. I zeroed in on a few heavenly coordinates to lift my sights above my physical pain: *When we see Him we shall be like Him. The perishable shall put on the imperishable—the corruptible, that which is incorruptible. That which is sown in weakness will be raised in power. He has given us an inheritance that can never perish, spoil or fade. If we suffer with Him, we shall reign with Him.*

It was all I needed. I opened my eyes and said out loud with a smile, "Come quickly, Lord Jesus."

A HEAVENLY PERSPECTIVE

But those who hope in the LORD will renew their strength. They will soar on wings like eagles; they will run and not grow weary, they will walk and not be faint.

—Isaiah 40:31

Physical affliction and emotional pain are, frankly, part of my daily routine. But I only stay me-centered long enough to release a few tears, blubber a few gripes, and that's it. I learned long ago that self-pity can be a deadly trap, and so I avoid it like the plague. I quickly move upward and onward.

Hardships are God's way of helping me to get my mind on the hereafter. And I don't mean the hereafter as a death wish, psychological crutch, or escape from reality. I mean "hereafter" as the true reality. And nothing beats rehearsing a few time-honored, well-worn verses of Scripture if you want to put reality into perspective. I look beyond the negatives and see the positives. . . .

I recall that pilgrims aren't supposed to feel at home on earth.

I remember the promise of a new body, heart, and mind.

I dream about reigning on earth and ruling in heaven.

I think about crowns and rewards and casting them all at Jesus' feet.

When these Scriptures strike that resonant chord in my heart, I tune into the melody and hold myself in the state of listening to heaven's music. Before I know it, the song lifts me, and I'm soaring on Spirit wings, breathing celestial air. I'm in heaven. It's a glorious vantage point from which to look down on my pain and problems.

Looking down on my problems from heaven's perspective, trials looked extraordinarily different. When viewed from its own level, my paralysis seemed like a huge, impassable wall; but when viewed from above, the wall appeared as a thin line, something that could be overcome. It was, I discovered with delight, a bird's-eye view. It was the view of Isaiah 40:31.

Eagles overcome the lower law of gravity by the higher law of flight, and what is true for birds is true for the soul. Souls that soar to heaven's heights on wings like eagles overcome the mud of earth that keeps us stuck to a temporal, limited perspective. If you want to see heaven's horizons, as well as place earth in your rearview mirror, all you need to do is stretch your wings (yes, you have wings, you don't need larger, better ones, you possess all that you need to gain a heavenly perspective on your trials) and consider your trials from heaven's realms. Like the wall that becomes a thin line, you are able to see the other side, the happier outcome.

The soul that mounts up to heaven's kingdom cannot fail to triumph. That's what happened to me. I was able to look beyond my "wall" to see where Jesus was taking me on my spiritual journey.

LORD, I'M THANKFUL FOR an eagle's eye view on the problems in my life. When you remind me to keep your higher perspective on situations, my attitudes and actions overcome the mud of earth and soar heavenward. May your eagle's eye view be mine today no matter what comes. ✐

LIGHT AND MOMENTARY TROUBLE

*For our light and momentary troubles
are achieving for us an eternal glory that
far outweighs them all.*

—*2 Corinthians 4:17*

Scripture mainly presents us with a view of life from the eternal perspective. What is transitory, such as physical pain, will not endure, but what is lasting, such as the eternal weight of glory accrued from that pain, will remain forever. Everything else—numbing heartache, deep disappointment, circumstances that seem topsy-turvy—everything else, no matter how real it seems to us on earth, is treated as inconsequential. Hardships are hardly worth noticing.

The apostle Peter had this perspective too when he wrote to Christian friends being flogged and beaten. "In this you greatly rejoice, though now for a little while you may have had to suffer grief in all kinds of trials" (1 Peter 1:6).

Rejoice? When you're being thrown to lions? The Christians to whom Peter was writing were suffering horribly under Nero, the Roman emperor. Peter expected them to view their problems as lasting . . . *a little while?* What sort of wristwatch was he using?

This kind of nonchalance about gut-wrenching suffering used to drive me crazy. Stuck in a wheelchair and staring out the window over the fields of our farm, I wondered, *Lord, how in the world can You consider my troubles light and momentary? I will never walk or run again. I will never use my hands. I've got a leaky leg bag . . . I smell like urine . . . my back aches . . . I'm trapped in front of this window. Maybe You see all of this achieving an eternal glory, but all I see is one awful day after the next of life in this stinking wheelchair!*

I did not buy the heavenly point of view. My pain screamed for my undivided attention, insisting, "Forget the future! What's God going to do *now*?" Time does that. It rivets your attention on temporal things and makes you live in the moment. And suffering doesn't make it any easier. It tightens the screw on the moment, making you anxious to find quick fix-its or escape hatches. That's what it was like as I pitied myself in my chair. When I read Romans 5:3, "rejoice in our sufferings," my first thought was, *Sure, God, I'll rejoice the day You get me out of this thing! And if You don't, what's going on? Are You poking fun at my paralysis? Trying to convince me I'm in spiritual denial? That my hurt and pain are imaginary?* When it came to my affliction being light and momentary, God was obviously using a different dictionary.

Years later the light dawned. The Lord hadn't used a different lexicon when He picked words like "light and momentary" to define earthly troubles. Even if it meant being sawn asunder, torn apart by lions, or plopped in a wheelchair for the rest of one's life. The Spirit-inspired writers of the Bible simply had a different perspective, an end-of-time view. Perspective changes everything.

THE END OF TIME VIEW

Why, you do not even know what will happen tomorrow. What is your life? You are a mist that appears for a little while and then vanishes.

—James 4:14

It's a matter of perspective. Some call it "the heavenly point of view." I like to refer to it as the "end-of-time view." This perspective separates what is transitory from what is lasting. "Therefore we do not lose heart," 2 Corinthians 4:16 says. The greater weight of eternal glory is clear:

The healing of that old ache.

Joy, eternal and ecstatic.

Being beautifully robed in righteousness.

Knowing Christ fully, my King and co-heir.

The final destruction of death, disease, and the devil. The vindication of His holy name. The restoration of all things under Christ.

These things outweigh thousands of afternoons of sweats and high blood pressure any day. They outweigh a lifetime of not feeling or moving. Mind you, I'm not saying that my paralysis is light in and of itself, it only *becomes* light in contrast to the far greater weight on the other side of the scale. And although I wouldn't normally call three decades in a wheelchair "momentary," it *is* when you realize that "you are a mist that appears for a little while and then vanishes" (James 4:14).

Scripture is constantly trying to get us to look at life this way. Our life is but a blip on the eternal screen. Pain will be erased by a greater understanding, it will be eclipsed by a glorious result. Something so superb, so grandiose is going to happen at the world's finale, that it will suffice for every hurt and atone for every heartache. It also helps to know that the state of suffering we are in here is necessary to reach the state we want (more accurately, God wants!) in heaven.

This is why Jesus spent so much energy emphasizing the end-of-time perspective. The Lord had come from heaven, and He knew how wonderful it was. Thus, He was always focusing on end results—the harvest of the crop, the fruit from the tree, the close of the day's labor, the profit from the investment, the house that stands the storm. He knew if we were to rejoice in our suffering, our fascination with the here and now would have to be subdued. How else could He say to those who mourn, "You are blessed"? How else could He tell the persecuted to be happy? How else could He remind His followers facing torture and death to "count it all joy"?

Nothing more radically altered the way I looked at my suffering than leapfrogging to this end-of-time vantage point. Heaven became my greatest hope. I knew the end result in heaven would exude a fragrant and glorious aroma: Christ in me, the hope of glory.

> **FATHER, I THANK YOU** that my life is but a mist that is vanishing swiftly. Thank you for your promises of greater blessing at the end of time. Help me to stand firm on those promises and say about my sufferings "These will pass and all will be worth it." ✍

HARDSHIP, HOPE AND HEAVEN

Praise be to the God and Father of our Lord Jesus Christ! In his great mercy he has given us new birth into a living hope through the resurrection of Jesus Christ from the dead, and into an inheritance that can never perish, spoil or fade—kept in heaven for you.

—1 Peter 1:3-4

So what is this connection between heaven and our hardships?

Although paralysis has aided me in my pilgrimage, it has not made me automatically holy. You could say the same about your own suffering. Pain and problems do not make one instantly obedient. For me, it has taken time. Time solves the dilemma of Romans 8:28, as well as all the other problems of evil, suffering, and pain. Time, in more ways than one.

You may not be paralyzed with a broken neck, but you could be paralyzed by other limitations. A broken heart. A broken home. A broken reputation. These things that presently scream for your undivided attention may close the doors to earthly satisfaction, but they can swing windows wide-open to a spirited hope of heaven.

Mind you, the closed doors—many of which have slammed in your face and crunched your fingers—are no accident. God wishes to instill within you a deep desire for your inheritance that can never perish, spoil, or fade, but in order to grip your heart, He will take drastic measures. You may not appreciate His *modus operandi* at first, but later, with an end-of-time perspective, you can be grateful for it.

Samuel Rutherford described the connection between heaven and hardships this way: "If you should see a man shut up in a closed room, idolizing a set of lamps and rejoicing in their light, and you wished to make him truly happy, you would begin by blowing out all his lamps; and then throw open the shutters to let in the light of heaven."

That's exactly what God did for me when He sent a broken neck my way. He blew out the lamps in my life that lit up the here and now and made it so captivating. The dark despair of total and permanent paralysis that followed wasn't much fun, but it sure made heaven come alive. And one day, when our Bridegroom comes back—probably when I'm right in the middle of lying down on my office sofa for the umpteenth time—God is going to throw open heaven's shutters. There's not a doubt in my mind that I'll be fantastically more excited and ready for it than if I were on my feet.

Suffering is no failure of God's plan. True, it is part of the curse, along with death, disease, and destruction. But before God comes back to close the curtain on suffering, it is meant to be redeemed. As Dorothy Sayers said, "Only in Christianity do we see a good God reaching down into what otherwise would be awful evil and wrench out of it positive good for us, and glory for Himself."

Hurrying the Heart
Toward Home

*My flesh and my heart may fail, but
God is the strength of my heart and my
portion forever.*

—*Psalm 73:26*

When I was on my feet, it would have been nice had I focused on heaven purely for Christ's sake, but forget that. Altruistic, yes. But realistic? No. Who wants to think about heaven when you've got things to do and places to go here?

It's the nature of the human beast. At least this beast. Some people have to break their necks in order to get their hearts on heavenly glories above, and I happen to be one of them. It was only after the permanency of my paralysis sank in, that heaven interested me.

You can appreciate this, especially if earth has broken your heart. You may be a mother who has lost her child in an accident, a son who has lost his father to cancer, or a husband whose wife has passed on to glory. These dear ones take with them a part of your heart that no one can replace. And since the pursuit of heaven is an occupation of the heart anyway, don't be surprised if you find yourself longing for heaven after you leave the graveside. If your heart is with your loved ones, and they are home with the Lord, then heaven is home for you too.

A broken heart leads to the true contentment of asking less of this life because more is coming in the next. The art of living with suffering is the art of readjusting your expectations in the here and now. There are simply some things I will *never have* because of this wheelchair. Such longings heighten my loneliness here on earth. The psalmist wrapped words around this loneliness in Psalm 73:25–26 when he said, "Whom have I in heaven but you? And being with you, I desire nothing on earth. My flesh and my heart may fail, but God is the strength of my heart and my portion forever."

But asking less is not a loss, and readjusting expectations is not a negative. It's good. When I was on my feet, big boisterous pleasures provided only fleeting satisfaction. In a wheelchair, satisfaction settles in as I sit under an oak tree on a windy day and delight in the rustle of leaves or sit by a fire and enjoy the soothing strains of a symphony. These smaller, less noisy pleasures are rich because, unlike the fun on my feet, these things yield patience, endurance, and a spirit of gratitude, all of which fits me further for eternity.

It is this yieldedness that gains you the most here on earth. You enjoy "a sincere heart in full assurance of faith" as it says in Hebrews 10:22, which in turn gives conviction to unseen divine realities and future divine fulfillments. You enjoy a new degree, a new release of energy at every point in your life as the eye of your soul is strengthened and spiritual understanding is quickened. A greater assurance of faith shows you that all things are, indeed, working together for good, and you realize without a doubt that the smallest of kind deeds done in Christ's name will result in a greater capacity to serve God in glory.

Suffering hurries the heart homeward.

SHARING IN CHRIST'S GLORY

*We share in his sufferings in order that
we may also share in his glory.*

—*Romans 8:17*

Just think. *Suppose you had never in your life known physical pain.*
No sore back, twisted ankle, or decayed molars. What if you
never had to use those crutches or that walker? How could you
appreciate the scarred hands with which Christ will greet you?

Yes, Jesus will be the only One in heaven who will bear the
scars of life on earth, the print of nails in His hands. We know
this because on His throne, the risen Christ appears "as a Lamb
that had been slain." And when we touch His scars, God will
give us at least a partial answer to the "Why?" questions about
our suffering, commenting to us, "Why not?"

If Jesus went through so much suffering to secure for us that
which we don't deserve, why did we complain when we endured on
earth only a tiny fraction of what He went through on our behalf?

In a way, I wish I could take to heaven my old, tattered Ever-
est & Jennings wheelchair. I would point to the empty seat and
say, "Lord, for decades I was paralyzed in this chair. But it
showed me how paralyzed You must have felt to be nailed to
Your Cross. My limitations taught me something about the lim-

itations You endured when You laid aside Your robes of state and put on the indignity of human flesh."

At that point, with my strong and beautiful glorified body, I might sit in it, rub the armrests with my hands, look up at Jesus, and add, "The weaker I felt in this chair, the harder I leaned on You. And the harder I leaned, the more I discovered how strong You are. Thank You, Jesus, for learning obedience in Your suffering. You gave me grace to learn obedience in mine."

Not only will I appreciate the scars of Christ, but also the scars of other believers. There I will see men and women that in the world were cut in pieces, burnt in flames, tortured and persecuted, eaten by beasts, and drowned in the seas—all for the love they had for the Lord. What a privilege it will be to stand near their ranks! But what a shame it would be if, in conversing with them, we could only shrug our shoulders and prattle, "Me? Suffer? Well, there was that time I had to endure the most insipid color of yellow on my living room walls . . . and, oh yes, my gallbladder surgery. Do you want to see my scars?"

Forgive me for being flippant, but perhaps we would bite our complaining tongues more often if we stopped to picture the scene in heaven. The examples of other suffering saints—people who considered it a privilege to bear their sufferings with grace so they might share in Christ's glory—are meant to inspire us upward on our heavenly journey home.

But if, instead, we stifled complaints and rejoiced in the privilege of participating in the sufferings of Christ, we will be overjoyed when His glory bursts on the scene.

SUFFERING PREPARES US

*That is why, for Christ's sake, I delight
in weaknesses, in insults, in hardships,
in persecutions, in difficulties. For when
I am weak, then I am strong.*

—*2 Corinthians 12:10*

Suppose you had never in your life known emotional pain. No stained reputation. No bruised feelings. No pangs of guilt. What if no one had ever offended you deeply? How could you adequately express your gratitude when you approach the Man of Sorrows who was acquainted with grief?

If you were never embarrassed or felt ashamed, you could never grasp how much He loved you when He endured the spit from soldiers, the spinelessness of His disciples, the callousness of the crowd, and the jeers from the mob. He took your shameful sins and made them His. All for the love of you.

Suppose you had never in your life known the struggle against sin. There's a distinct connection between heaven and this struggle. It is rare to find believers who, for the sake of heaven, purify themselves. But I want to be one of them, don't you? I want to sweep my conscience clean and jerk open every closet in my heart that hides a skeleton. It's painful to sit this close to self-scrutiny and cut away every sin that entangles. But it's what the Lord requires.

How could we be thrilled to meet the Lord face-to-face after clinging on earth to the very sins for which He died? It is impossible to hold onto sinful habits while, at the same time, holding onto the desire to touch the nail-scarred hands of Christ. No one can hope for heaven while consciously clutching onto sins he knows to be offensive. True, holy living is rugged and demanding, but its heavenly rewards are precious.

Yes, it's a struggle. And the entire chapter seven of Romans assures us holy living will always be a struggle. But think of it as the best way of showing your love to Christ!

A curious thing will happen if you view your suffering this way. Once you see your affliction as a preparation to meet God, you won't be quick to call it "suffering" again. Even though I have rough moments in my wheelchair, for the most part I consider my paralysis a gift. Just as Jesus exchanged the meaning of the Cross from a symbol of torture to one of hope and salvation, He gives me the grace to do the same with my chair. If a cross can become a blessing, so can a wheelchair.

I'm inspired by Madame Guyon who, although locked away in the depths of a French dungeon for many years, wrote, "I have no desire that my imprisonment should end before the right time; I love my chains."

When you meet Jesus face-to-face, your loyalty in your hardships will give you something tangible, something concrete to offer Him in return. For what proof could you bring of your love and faithfulness if this life left you totally unscarred?

> Before the winds that blow do cease,
> Teach me to dwell within Thy calm:
> Before the pain has passed in peace,
> Give me, my God, to sing a psalm.
>
> — Amy Carmichael

OVERWHELMING SUFFERING

Record my lament; list my tears on your
scroll—are they not in your record?

—Psalm 56:8

*O*kay, I'll accept this connection between hardship and heaven, but what if the hardship is insurmountable? Overwhelming? Unbearable?

"I'm a Christian," Lisa said. "Why do I have to go through all this?"

I leaned my head against the receiver and wondered, for the thousandth time, what to say. I'd had many years in a wheelchair. Lisa, only a few. I'm paralyzed from the shoulders down, but Lisa is paralyzed from the neck down. She can't even breathe on her own. How can one deal with so much frustration and affliction? How could I expect her to grasp the things that had taken me ages to understand? What could I give or say to help? This young respirator-dependent quadriplegic is thrust out into a no-man's-land, way ahead of the front-line trenches where most of us suffer.

Her questions were not the "why?" of the clenched fist sort, but the "why?" of a searching heart. Lisa was actually wondering how to live, how to view her affliction as meaningful.

"I want to understand . . . I don't want to live . . . my life in vain. . . ." she breathed into the phone.

For the next hour, I slowly tried to lift her sights beyond the impassable wall of her hospital room. I began with the basics (which are really not so basic) and shared how her paralysis could become the best place from which to know God. Perfect stillness is not always available to those who would appreciate it most, and often not appreciated by those who have it. Lisa had a long way to go before she could learn how to be comfortable in her enforced stillness, but the softness in her voice assured me she was on her way.

"Enough has been wasted in your life, Lisa," I said. "Don't waste anymore of it. And don't worry about finding answers. I don't think they would satisfy you at this point anyway. Just use the time you've got, the stillness you're experiencing . . . use it to get to know God. Talk to Him in prayer, and let Him talk to you in His Word."

Lisa told me she would start doing just that, especially when I told her that the faintest prayers of those who suffer reach more deeply into God's heart. At that point, I imagined angels in heaven kicking up their heels and rejoicing. This vent-dependent quadriplegic who will lie in bed and spend long moments in prayer may not realize it, but she will be doing the work of angels. After all, there are angels in heaven who do nothing but praise God, such as the seraphim who proclaim day and night before the Lord, "Holy, Holy, Holy!"

THANK YOU, LORD, for the strength—your strength—I have found in suffering. Thank you that in a small way my trials help me identify with your suffering on the cross for me. Help me to see the hard things of my life with eyes of grace and to recognize the blessings that my sufferings bring.

THE GREATER GLORY

Rejoice that you participate in the sufferings of Christ, so that you may be overjoyed when His glory is revealed.

—*1 Peter 4:13*

There is a direct relationship between earth's suffering and heaven's glory. God wants those who suffer greatly to receive even greater glory. I'm not glorifying suffering here. Problems are real, and I'm not denying that suffering hurts. I'm just denying that it *matters* in the grander scheme of things. It is light and momentary *compared* with what our response is producing for us in heaven—yes, suffering is pivotal to future glory.

Let me explain. The greatest suffering that ever occurred happened on the Cross. And the greatest glory ever given in response to suffering was the glory ascribed to Christ when He ascended. He suffered "death on a cross . . . *therefore* God exalted him to the highest place" (Philippians 2:8–9).

When the mother of James and John approached the Lord and asked if her sons could please enjoy a position of prominence in the kingdom of heaven, the Lord replied, "You don't know what you're asking." Then He said to her sons, "Can you drink the cup I am going to drink?"

"We can," they answered.

Jesus said to them, "You will indeed drink from my cup."

The Lord inferred that if His followers were to share in His glory, they would also have to share in His sufferings. And the deeper the suffering, the higher the glory. This is why the apostle Peter could say that to the degree one suffers, keep on rejoicing, we rejoice on earth so that we may be overjoyed in heaven.

Does this mean that those who suffer greatly, yet nobly, will have a bigger halo? A shinier face? No, but it does mean that they will enjoy a greater capacity to serve God in heaven.

I'm sure there will be times when Lisa (my quadriplegic friend) will smirk—like I did—as she reads Romans 8:18, "I consider that our present sufferings are not worth comparing with the glory that will be revealed in us." Like me, she will go through cycles, thinking, *Is the Bible being flippant about my lot in life?* But as long as she keeps focused on the basics—being still and knowing God through prayer and Scripture—she will remain on the high road home. She will be more devoted to the future than the present. More devoted to the spiritual than the physical. And more devoted to eternal realities than temporal ones.

> The clock has stopped. The universe has flashed
> and cracked. The flood has swept the dam.
> Bright angels sift like gold dust from the gash,
> heralding invitations of the lamb:
> "Arise ye hobbling, tattered, orphaned, blind,
> Ye maimed in spirit, measured without merit,
> by men cast off as useless. Rise and find
> the crown, the throne, the birthright to inherit.
>
> —Douglas Kaine McKelvey

DON'T LEAVE YET!

*Be very careful, then, how you live—
not as unwise but as wise, making the
most of every opportunity, because the
days are evil.*

—Ephesians 5:15-16

The firmer my heart becomes anchored in heaven, the more I want to go there. Now.

It has nothing to do with being tired of sitting down or getting cricks in my neck from holding up my head all day. It's just that less of my heart is here, and more of it is there. I identify with the apostle Paul who said in Philippians 1:21, "For me to live is Christ, and to die is gain. Now if I am to go on living, this will mean fruitful labor for me. Yet what shall I choose? I don't know. I am torn between the two: I desire to depart and be with Christ which is better by far . . . but it is more necessary for you that I remain in the body."

Like Paul, I often debate the pros and cons of life. But also like him, my earthly life is meant to be one of discontentment. I am torn between the two. I desire to depart. Since my heart has already gone ahead, I long to follow it home. But it is more necessary that I remain in the body. For others.

I'm not talking about you being an inspiration. It's more than that . . . it's a mystery. God somehow strengthens others by your faithfulness. What's more, it's all being credited to your account. The apostle Paul said so in Philippians 1:25–26 when he told a bunch of guys his example inspired, "I will continue with all of you so that through my being with you again your joy in Christ Jesus will overflow on account of me." Did you get that part about "on account of me?" If good things happen to others because of your example, God chalks it up on your record.

I had a friend named Denise when I was in the hospital. She laid in bed for eight years, blind and paralyzed. She hung in there despite the odds.

Denise died after eight years in that bed. My human logic said, "God, You should have taken her home to heaven sooner what did all her striving accomplish for the handful of nurses who happened to know her?" But then I read a verse in Ephesians 3:10 that says God uses our lives like a blackboard upon which He teaches lessons about Himself. And He does it for the benefit of angels and demons—maybe not people, but quadrillions of unseen beings.

Something dynamic is happening in heaven right now. Angels and demons are learning new things about God. It happens when believers allow their painful circumstances to be the platform from which their souls rise to heavenly heights. Every day that we go on living in these bodies means fruitful labor—for us, for others, for the glory of God, and for the heavenly hosts.

FATHER, THE PROMISE OF a future rest reminds me that now is not the time to rest, but rather to work. Help me make the most of every day for your glory as I follow the journey home. ✒

ONWARD AND UPWARD

*For just as the sufferings of Christ flow
over into our lives, so also through Christ
our comfort overflows. If we are distressed,
it is for your comfort and salvation; if we
are comforted, it is for your comfort,
which produces in you patient endurance
of the same sufferings we suffer.*

—*2 Corinthians 1:5-6*

Suffering always drives us in deeper and up higher. Always
onward and upward into the heart of heaven.

Lisa and I continued to keep in touch. She settled into a living situation with a friend and began to attend a local college.
She got involved with her church and started going to Bible
study. After five years, we lost contact. I wasn't worried about
her, though, because she seemed to be on a steady path.

This year, however, I got the shock of my life when, after I
finished speaking at a conference, a young woman hooked up
to a ventilator wheeled up to me with a confident smile. I knew
immediately who she was. The light in her eyes assured me this
was the same young woman. She was happily heading for home
and making the most of every day on the way.

Had Madame Guyon been able to reach across the centuries to Lisa (confined in her own set of bolts and bars), she would congratulate her with these words penned from her dark dungeon: "What gain has been made compared to the little that has been lost! You will have lost 'the creature' in order to gain 'the Creator.' You will have lost your nothingness in order to gain all things. You will be boundless, for you will have inherited God!"

Lisa and I have seen the future, and the future is us. A glorious future for those who, for Christ's sake, suffer valiantly.

Yours is a glorious future too. God has placed suffering in your life to remind you that heaven is not only for the future; it is for now, for this present moment. Heaven is meant to bless your path and be a source of strength in your suffering today. Valiantly welcome it and greet it.

No heaven can come to us unless our hearts find rest in it today. Take heaven. No peace lies in the future that is not hidden in this precious little instant. Take peace. The gloom of the world is but a shadow. Behind it, within our reach, is joy. Life is so generous a giver, but we, judging its gifts by their coverings, cast them away as ugly or heavy or hard. Remove the covering and you will find beneath it a living splendor, woven of love and wisdom and power. Welcome it, greet it, and touch the angel's hand that brings it.

EVERYTHING WE CALL A TRIAL, a sorrow, a duty: believe me, that angel's hand is there, the gift is there, and the wonder of an overshadowing Presence. Life is so full of meaning and purpose, so full of beauty beneath its covering, that you will find earth but cloaks your heaven. Courage, then, to claim it, that is all! But courage you have, and the knowledge that we are pilgrims wending through unknown country on our way home.

—Fra Angelico

PART 10

HOMEWARD BOUND

Socrates, being asked what countryman he was, answered, "I am a citizen of the whole world." But ask a Christian what countryman he is, and he will answer, "I am a citizen of all heaven."

— WILLIAM SECKER

Can you believe that sunset?"

My friends paused, and together we stood, quietly, face-on into the color. It washed us in its glowing tone, touching us like the finger of

Midas and making our group a single and silent statue of gold. We were bound together in a timeless moment that we knew was slipping away even as we tried to hold on to it. Drink it all in, we seemed to understand, this won't last forever.

As the colors peaked, golden rays shot up from behind the mountain just as the last vestige of sun slid beneath its crest. Then, it was gone. Finished.

We watched the sky darken and threaten as fog from the ocean crept up over the hills. I shivered, we said good-bye, and went our separate ways. Getting into my van, I remembered a favorite line from Amy Carmichael: "We will have all of eternity to celebrate the victories, and only a few hours before sunset in which to win them."

Miss Carmichael knew a lot about the Christian life—and a lot about sunsets. She knew the colors of the fading sun mesmerize us with their beauty, making us stand still and almost believe in timeless moments. Then, in the next second, the lingering pink and gold vanish.

Why am I always surprised at how fast sunsets disappear?

Then again, I'm always amazed at how fast life disappears. I watch a sunset, get in the van, drive away, stop at the gas station, the market, help Ken fix dinner, and then collapse in bed long after dark. Next morning I'm up and at it again. My life will be gone in a flash, in the twinkling of an eye. Suddenly—just like that—it will be over. Finished. The fading beauty of all the good things in life will disappear.

DRINK IT ALL IN . . . this won't last forever. ✒

TWILIGHT YEARS

I tell you the truth, anyone who will not receive the kingdom of God like a little child will never enter it.

—Luke 18:17

No one appreciates sunsets like my mother. Lindy, as her friends call her, is like me in that she will put everything on hold to watch a sassy sunset. During the summer, her early evening ritual includes pulling up a chair and sipping coffee on the back porch of her condominium to watch the sun disappear below Sinepuxent Bay on the eastern shore of Maryland. Then she will watch the twilight give way to a thousand twinkling stars that stretch from horizon to horizon. She loves looking up and always telephones me to remind me when there's a full moon.

Mother is aware of how short the days are. At eighty-one years of age, she has seen ten thousand sunsets and understands that even the brightest day is sure to have its twilight. For her, the shadows are falling longer, thicker, and faster, and the warmth is going out of the air. Her strongest hours of building with gold, silver, and precious stones are waning as the afternoon of her life is passing. Lindy knows she is approaching twilight. But even in her twilight, even though Mother seems grand and old, she is so . . . *young!*

I'm convinced it's because she keeps looking up and focusing on something far beyond her many birthdays. After all, to live in the heavenlies is to live in a kind of timelessness. People who look up and see beyond the encroaching years enlarge their souls with eternity. They have about them the air of something eternal, not temporal. They know every year draws them closer to heaven, which, in turn, instills more youth into their hearts.

You don't have to convince my mother, and you don't have to twist the arm of my friend, Alice McIntire. Although definitely in her twilight, she won't tell her age because, as she puts it, "Any woman who tells her age, will tell anything." Her spunk, humor, and style amaze me, and I once said to Alice, "You must be really looking forward to heaven," to which she replied, "Oh, honey, yes, but I hope I stay around for Jesus' return. I never like to miss a good party."

Alice keeps looking up. This is why she stays so young (as does my mother). Every Christian who keeps looking up stretches his heart's capacity for heaven. They don't seem old, they are young.

I'm not ninety or in my eighties, but I identify. I feel so young inside, somewhere around the age of twelve or thirteen. As though I were a little girl. A girl like my mother who still bundles up to run outside and gaze at the moon. We feel young when we forget the temporal and focus on the eternal—that's what children do who have no concept of time, and of such is the kingdom of heaven.

IT'S HARD TO ADMIT it sometimes, Lord, but I'm growing older. I sense the days to win victories for you are growing shorter too. Enlarge my soul with the timelessness of a child and let me see the important, eternal things of heaven beyond these encroaching years. ✒

A PAINFUL PASSAGE

*Precious in the sight of the LORD is the
death of his saints.*

—*Psalm 116:15*

It may be brighter at twilight, but not necessarily easier.

That final passage for my mother may be swift and sweet, but there's no guarantee. For many, the passage is ugly and painful.

Christians shouldn't glamorize death. Death is Satan's last-ditch effort, and he's going to make it as awful as he can. But God has the last word. Resurrection.

I think of Corrie ten Boom, the Dutch woman who was sent to a Nazi concentration camp for hiding Jewish families. Years after Tante Corrie's release, her companion, Pam Rosewell, sat by her bedside when she was old and stroke-stricken. Watching Corrie's mind and body waste away to a thin shadow of her former self, she wondered why the Lord didn't take Tante Corrie home sooner. But Pam observed after the funeral of her elderly friend, "Every day she lived was a victory over the devil . . . he would have had her die fifty years earlier in Ravensbruck, but just the act of living, without doing a thing, just breathing life in and out was a triumph. If her final years had not influenced any person on earth and if the only reason the Lord allowed her to remain on earth was to make a silent daily statement to the principalities in heavenly places that 'Jesus is victor,' then it was an important silence indeed."

I look at my own degenerating body and wonder how I will approach that final passage. Will it be short and sweet? Or long and agonizing? Will my husband be able to take care of me? Or will my quadriplegia better suit me for a nursing home? It's not so much I'm afraid of death as dying.

Whether it's painfully prolonged or a peaceful passing in the night, I'm strangely comforted by the thought that the servant shouldn't expect to suffer less than his Master. There is no holy peace with death. Even earth will convulse in upheaval in its final birth pangs before the new heavens and new earth. All seeds—whether a plant, a person, or a planet—must die. But then, the harvest.

I AM STANDING UPON the seashore. A ship at my side spreads her white sails to the morning breeze and starts for the blue ocean. She is an object of beauty and strength, and I stand and watch her until at length she hangs like a speck of white cloud just where the sea and sky come down to mingle with each other. Then someone at my side says: "There! She's gone." Gone where? Gone from my sight—that is all. She is just as large in mast and hull and spar as she was when she left my side, and just as able to bear her load of living freight to the place of destination. Her diminished size is in me, not in her; and just at the moment when someone at my side says, "There! She's gone," there are other eyes watching her coming, and other voices ready to take up the glad shout, "There she comes!" And that is Dying!

—Author Unknown

BETWEEN DEATH AND RESURRECTION

*Teach us to number our days aright, that
we may gain a heart of wisdom.*

—*Psalm 90:12*

The glowing sunset behind the coastal mountains stopped me in my tracks. I sat by my van in the parking lot and watched the hues shift and deepen from vivid lilac to pink and then a fiery red. A show-off sunset it was, a sassy kaleidoscope, teasing, inviting me to follow it over the horizon. It was another one of those heaven-inspired moments wooing me not only over the horizon, but home. I knew I couldn't follow. For now, I could only sit and enjoy.

Days are fleeting, hours are fading, and before you know it, we will no longer have the chance to prove our love to Jesus with our obedience. We won't have the time to get back on track. To build with gold, silver, and precious stones.

The sun will have set.

Tante Corrie (and other believers who have died) are not diminished while they are presently in heaven. They gained immeasurably the instant they crossed from the land of the dying to the land of the living. Second Corinthians 5:8 explains that "to be away from the body [is to be] at home with the Lord." They are not present with the Lord in some soul-sleep right now; they are "at home" with Him in the best sense of the word. They are alive, awake, aware, and full of the joy of having come home. Home where they fit, feel warm and welcomed, a place where they belong. Who can begin to measure the fullness of the meaning of that word "home"!

There's another way that departed saints are not diminished and the clue is given in Luke 16:19–31. Jesus relays not a parable, but an amazing real-life occurrence after the death of a beggar named Lazarus and a rich man. The rich man was very conscious of his hellish surroundings as well as the condition of his brothers who still remained on earth, and he wanted desperately to warn his family. He felt, saw, prayed, remembered, and desired. My point? If lost souls can feel and care, how much more can those who have died in the faith!

How deeply they must feel and pray and see. How fervent must be their love. Love does not die; it cannot die because it cannot fail. Love is a part of a departed saint's being, not his body, but his person. Could it be that our loved ones in glory are able to love us now? Pray for us now?

In heaven, we do not lose, for "to die is gain." We aren't less, we're more. When we die, we're not in some soul-sleep of a stupor, not purgatory, and we're certainly not unconscious. We are at home with the Lord. Home!

HELP ME, FATHER, as I step out in obedience and send my heart ahead to heaven. Strike that resonant chord in my inner being as I take that step that lets me know I am home-ward bound. ✒

RESURRECTION AND REST

There remains, then, a Sabbath-rest for the people of God.

—*Hebrews 4:9*

My mother-in-law recently purchased a family grave plot at a cemetery. She would not sign the papers, however, until Ken and I looked at the lot and gave our approval.

I trekked to Forest Lawn with Ken and looked at my grave site located in a section called "Murmuring Pines." While the realtor and my mother-in-law conferred over the papers, I looked around at the hundreds of tombstones. It suddenly struck me that I was sitting on the exact spot where my body will rise, should I die before Christ comes. Resting on that grassy hillside did more to ignite the reality of the Resurrection than hearing sermons or reading essays on the subject. One day actual beings will return to actual graves and reunite to rise.

One day, the Resurrection.

And then, heaven.

Then, rest.

Not the rest of inactivity, but rest from the pain, the weariness, and the disappointment. I may only be cresting middle age, but like many of my friends who have toiled for years, I'm ready for a rest. No more wrestling against sin. No more prying the world's suction cups off my heart. No knock-down-drag-out fights with the devil. No collapsing in bed after an exhausting day only to snatch a few hours before you are up and at it again.

This thought alone makes the earthly toil not only bearable, but lighter. I can remember how, after hours of riding my horse to check gates and fences, my weary mount would be wet with sweat, her head hanging low. I had to urge her to put one tired hoof in front of another. Then as soon as she caught a whiff of home or recognized the fences of her own pasture, her ears would pick up and her pace would quicken. The nearer we came to the barn, the more eager her trot. After a quick unsaddling, she would joyfully roll in the dirt and take long deep drinks from the trough. How good it feels for a beast to be home, to be able to rest. How good it will feel for us to rest, to be at home.

Maybe the writers of the Bible—some who had scars on their bodies from stonings, others whose joints were stiff from chains that chafed—had this sweet rest in mind, a rest that perked them up and quickened their pace. They wrote vigorous encouragements like, "Let us, therefore, make every effort to enter that rest" and "Seeing that the days are short, make every effort . . . " and "Redeem the time for the days are evil." The weary labor for them seemed featherweight compared with the glorious rest into which they were about to enter.

LORD, THANK YOU FOR the promise of a heavenly body and conscience free from sin. Just knowing that one day I'll have the promises of heaven makes this earthly life not only bearable, but lighter. I praise you for your victory over my sin and the promised sweet rest of heaven that quickens my pace in service for you. ✒

SEIZE THE DAY!

*Therefore, as we have opportunity, let us
do good to all people, especially to those
who belong to the family of believers.*

—*Galatians 6:10*

I believe we are in the twilight of our hardships as well as the twilight of the world's history. I believe the days are short. My closing words for you are "Make the most of every opportunity" (Colossians 4:5). It is what Alice and my mother are doing, and it is what Tante Corrie did those last painful years of her life. If we could hear it from the lips of Amy Carmichael herself, perhaps we would sense the urgency of winning triumphs for Christ in these last few hours before the sun disappears.

Let me read one final and powerful verse from 2 Peter 3:8. It begins, "But do not forget this one thing, dear friends." You probably know from your days in Sunday school that what Peter is about to say is ultra-important, like Jesus saying, "Verily, verily!" And he continues, "With the Lord a day is like a thousand years, and a thousand years are like a day."

That verse is so key. We all recognize the old adage that God looks at the last two thousand years as only a couple of days gone by, but how many of us ever consider the next half of the verse? The part about seeing each day as like a thousand years? It's a little like divine geometry, a mathematical formula assuring us that each day is a chance to invest in a thousand years worth of eternity. God gives us a twenty-four-hour slice of time in which to make the most of every opportunity, opportunities that will have eternal repercussions.

The way we spend the hours and moments counts. It counts far more than we realize.

I'm not saying that every day here exactly equals one thousand years there. Remember, heaven has a different kind of time. Time just *is* in heaven. My purpose in using 2 Peter 3:8 was simply to give heavenly meaning to our earthly hours.

Little wonder Psalm 90:12 says, "Teach us to number our days aright, that we may gain a heart of wisdom." *This* is the kind of wisdom God wants you to apply to your twenty-four-hour slices of time. This is the kind of wisdom that sends your heart on ahead to heaven.

Oh, if we could only realize how short life is. James 4:14 says, "What is your life? You are a mist that appears for a little while and then vanishes." And if we need another nudge, Isaiah 40:6–7 says, "All men are like grass. The grass withers and the flowers fall, because the breath of the Lord blows on them. Surely the people are grass." Therefore make every effort. The days are evil. Redeem the time.

Make the most of your moments.

LORD, HELP ME TO use the few hours left to me in this world to gain heavenly victories. Show me how I can make the most of every opportunity you send my way. Kindle a fire of urgency in my heart to win triumphs for you. ✒

COME HOME!

Instead, they were longing for a better country—a heavenly one. Therefore God is not ashamed to be called their God, for he has prepared a city for them.

—Hebrews 11:16

Just writing the last few pages has invigorated my excitement over how like the Rock of Gibraltar heaven is. I get tickled thinking about how rock-solid real heaven is, and how much of a home—much more so than earth—it will be. On some days, I feel as though I might be called Home any moment.

I had this "let's go home" feeling when I used to play in the woods beyond our backyard. As soon as I got home from elementary school, and while Mom was preparing dinner, I would put my things in my room and race out the back door to play tag with Kathy and a few neighborhood kids. Our play was so much fun that an hour would go by and I'd hardly realize it. I knew that soon Mother would call us home.

I rather enjoyed hearing the sound of Daddy's or Mom's voice through cupped hands, shouting my name. No sooner did I hope they'd call when I would hear the familiar ding-ding-a-ling-ding of the dinner bell by the back door.

"Supper's ready . . . time to come home!"

It's odd how I can still hear Mother's voice. The echo of the bell, the haunting sound through the woods, the joy about to break open my heart for the love of home, the warmth of family—not to mention fried chicken and mashed potatoes by a glowing fire in the dining room. And often during summer, after the table was cleared and dessert was over, we'd sit in the backyard and watch the sun go down.

And then, we'd wait until the stars came out, singing hymns and counting the constellations. It was all I could hope for as a kid. And here I am an adult, still looking beyond Ursa Major, singing heaven's melodies, and winning victories until earth's twilight gives way to the dawn of eternity.

Most of the things that have deeply possessed my soul have been echoes that have died away as soon as they caught my ear. But the echo of that dinner bell, now, many years later, has not died but is swelling into the sound itself.

When that happens to any of us, when those tantalizing glimpses, those promises never quite fulfilled, find broader, more complete fulfillment in our maturing years, then we know we've found what we've longed for. Beyond every possibility of a doubt, we would say, "Here at last is the thing I was made for . . . this is the healing of the old ache." That's why for me, the echoes are getting louder. They resonate with the rich, full, and deep tones of Someone calling just a short distance away.

> Come Home, come Home,
>   Ye who are weary, come Home;
> Earnestly, tenderly, Jesus is calling,
>   Calling, O sinner, come Home!

—Will L. Thompson

My Heart's Longing . . .
For You

Until now you have not asked for anything in my name. Ask and you will receive, and your joy will be complete.

—*John 16:24*

Years ago when I became paralyzed in a diving accident, my world was reduced to the basics. Lying for two years in a hospital bed on starched sheets surrounded by starched hospital workers, I lived in a sterile vacuum, doing little more than eating, breathing, and sleeping. I had all the time in the world to ask questions of God.

Perhaps friends who visited me thought I was being too philosophical. But they weren't faced with the larger-than-life questions that were plaguing me: "What is the meaning to life?" and "Where are we all heading?" Haunted and hurting, I realized there had to be more to life than just existing.

That's when I came face-to-face with the God of the Bible. I decided it was better to throw my questions at Him rather than shrug my shoulders and turn away. Those two years in the hospital were like one long question-and-answer session. What is the meaning to life? To know and glorify God. Where are we all heading? To enjoy Him forever . . . at least for those who know Him.

My heart's longing is that you know and enjoy Him forever too. And if your heart has been warmed by the things you've read on these pages, if you sense in them the ring of truth, then it is God who is saying to you, "Come home, come home . . . ye who are weary, come home."

The first step in the right direction Home begins with a prayer, honest and from the heart, to invite Jesus to be the Lord of your life. The next step in the right direction is to find a church where you can share your newfound affection for the Lord Jesus with other like-hearted believers in Him who center their faith around the Bible as God's Word. Step-by-step, you will grow to know Him better and to enjoy Him more.

I look forward to the day when our journey Home will end on the other side of those gates of pearl. When you get there, let's do heaven, and until then, let's do all we can to help other hearts get Homeward bound.

If you wish to be certain that you're homeward bound to heaven, and not hell, then feel free to borrow the following words and make them your personal prayer . . .

> **LORD JESUS, I REALIZE** I have lived my life far from You. I see now how my sin has separated me from You. Please come into my life—my heart, mind, and spirit—and make me the person You want me to be. Forgive me for living away from You all these years. Help me to turn from my old ways to Your new and righteous ways. I invite You to be Lord of my life and thank You for the difference You will make. Amen.

We want to hear from you. Please send your comments about this book to us in care of the address below. Thank you.

GRAND RAPIDS, MICHIGAN 49530

www.zondervan.com